D1044852

LIFE'S A MARATHON

Three Choices to Overcome Adversity and Achieve Greater Victory from a Three-Time Cancer Conqueror Who had to Relearn How to Walk and Became the Seven Continent Marathon Man

MATT JONES

PUBLISHED BY: Matt Jones International

PRINTED IN THE UNITED STATES OF AMERICA

WHAT OTHERS ARE SAYING ABOUT MATT JONES AND HIS STRATEGIES

"Matt Jones is a true champion and his story inspires others to be a true champion."

—**George Brett,** Baseball Hall of Famer, World Series Champion, Member of the exclusive 3,000 hits club

"Matt Jones is a speaker who entertains, enlightens, and creates an unforgettable experience for the audience."

—**Joe Theismann,** Legendary NFL World Champion Quarterback, NFL Football TV Commentator, Featured in the Hit Movie, The Blind Side

"Great job, Matt."

—**Bill Self,** Head coach Kansas Jayhawks, 2008 NCAA Men's Basketball National Champions

"You are my Hero!"

—**Wayne Dyer,** Internationally renowned author of over 30 Books including *"Your Erroneous Zones"* which as sold over 35 million copies

"Matt Jones speaks in a voice that transforms lives. His life example moves audiences of all kinds. He is truly one of the most gifted speakers I ever had the honor of working with, mentored, or sharing the stage with, I highly recommend Matt to speak at any occasion."

—**Les Brown,** "The World's Leading Motivational Speaker," Recipient of the National Speakers Association's CPAE Speaker Hall of Fame (NSA's highest award for speaking excellence)

"Matt has a wonderful ability to inspire and motivate you to overcome any obstacle and achieve any goal."

—**Brian Tracy,** Top selling author of over 45 books and legendary speaker who has addressed over 4,000,000 people in over 40 countries.

"Matt Jones is a gifted speaker and a master at motivation. Thank you, Matt, for sharing you remarkable story. Your message and passion will inspire audiences everywhere to achieve their own limitless success."

—**Barbara Niven,** TV Icon and Actress Known for roles in, "The Bold and the Beautiful," "One Life to Live," and "Pensacola: Wings of Gold"

"Matt Jones at a young age tapped into the universal power that is available to all. His story is proof of what is possible for our lives. He has a transformational message that is life changing."

—**Dr. Catherine Ponder,** One of America's foremost inspirational authors Author of the classic and international bestselling book, *"The Dynamic Laws of Prosperity"*

"Matt is an incredible speaker who speaks from the heart. You need to hear his message. I highly recommend Matt for your next event."

—**James Malinchak,** Featured on ABC's Hit TV Show Secret Millionaire, founder of www.BigMoneySpeaker.com

"Matt Jones proved to be a phenomenal closing keynote for our conference this year. He was exactly what we were looking for to conclude our conference with positivity and high energy! He did an excellent job of weaving his highly inspirational personal story along with practical and life-changing strategies for our attendees to take with them. Matt delivers an important message in a personal, memorable, and impactful way. I highly recommend him and know that he will bring great value to your event as he did to ours."

—**Sarah Carter,** Meeting Planners International Cascadia Educational Conference Chair

"Matt's presentation was outstanding! He has a phenomenal and inspiring story, which he presents in a dynamic and memorable way. We were very pleased with our choice of having Matt as our closing speaker. His talk allowed us to end our conference on a high note! I am glad that we booked Matt as our closing speaker. He did a great job!"

—**Steve Liechty,** Wyoming Recreation and Parks Association Conference Chair

"Your evaluations were extremely positive and some of the comments included:

> Excellent presentation! Matt was a dynamic speaker with a great leadership message.
> Great motivator and his humor kept us hooked!
> I could have listened to him all day.

I truly do appreciate how easy it was to work with you. You were prompt on any request we sent, generous with your time with our delegates and we very much appreciated the energy and enthusiasm you brought to our program."

—**Ginger Newman,** Director of Communication and Training, Wyoming Association of Municipalities

"I heard nothing but fabulous things about your two presentations. Having the opportunity to hear you inspire the crowd and tell your personal story was a truly an honor. What a memorable event! You had incredible energy and kept the room interested and engaged. I highly recommend Matt to anyone looking for a keynote speaker."

—**Leslie Adkins,** CAP-OM, International Association Administrate Professionals WA-AK Division Vice President

"Matt was fabulous! He rocked our opening session and engaged the audience from the beginning. His presentation was quite a high-energy way to start our conference and exactly what we were looking for. Through his powerful story, unique insights, and high energy, everyone in the room was positively influenced. We could not have asked for a better choice of a keynote speaker. He got us to laugh, get out of our seats, and absorb his wisdom. One of the best parts of the talk was the reminder of the difference we make in the lives of patients. This further made his inspiring story even more relevant to our event. The feedback we received was exceptional; I highly recommend Matt Jones as a speaker."

—**Karen J. Wilson,** President, Health Information Management Systems Society, Alabama Chapter

"Thank you Matt for making our day so rewarding. Your keynote presentation was the high point of a wonderful day of learning. Your session had the highest overall rating of other highly rated sessions. You were able to connect with our group of Human Resource Support Staff from the opening remarks and kept them engaged until the very end. Your story was heartwarming and hit very close to home among our group of HR Support Staff who face huge challenges at work every day. Your story motivates us to appreciate our 86,400 seconds of life each day and reminds us not to get overwhelmed with daily challenges and that they can become manageable by approaching the step by step using the strategies you shared."

—**Terry Serbin,** Executive Director, Michigan Chapter of American Association of School Personnel Administrators (MASPA)

"What a wonderful experience! You were a tremendous inspiration to my team. When I looked around the room, I saw tears and then moments of joy later. I think your speech is one that everyone can be lifted and inspired by. In these challenging times, it is imperative that companies empower their associates with positive "can do" attitudes. Your energy and enthusiasm in contagious! You bring uniqueness to your presentation that I have not seen before. I know that lives will be changed and attitudes improved because of your coaching style. Thanks again for sharing your tremendous success story with others!"

—**Sara D'Elia,** Vice President of Operations, Mesa Management

"It was awesome having Matt Jones kick off our meeting this past month. His magnetism lights up a room and carries over into a dynamic and inspiring presentation. His against all odds story resonated with our group and provided real life examples of handling the stresses/challenges especially as we work with patients and healthcare providers. His story is one of that would inspire any audience. He was very easy to work with before the presentation and felt like we got great value in his partnering with us for our meeting."

—**David A. Nye,** Chairman, Education Committee,
Georgia Medical Group Management Association

"The Arizona Multi-housing Association was honored to have Mr. Jones present at our annual Education Conference and Trade Show. The valuable insights that he shared with our membership translate into the current and future successes of our industry professionals. Matt's high energy went perfect with our "Rock' n" theme to jump-start his event! Thanks again!"

—**Rob Schmitz,** Manager of Education,
Arizona Multi-housing Association

"You were a true joy to work with for out IIANC Young Agent Sales & Leadership Boot Camp! Reading through the surveys I am only seeing, "exceeding my expectations," "great energy," "what a story," "very empowering" and "thank you for laughter!" Again, thank you for being so easy to work with from a planning stand point as well as a dynamic speaker to our Future Leaders of IIANC!"

—**Michelle Streath,** Director of Meetings and Events,
Independent Insurance Agents of North Carolina

"Matt Jones provided the perfect talk for our members. His message of the outside stuff not mattering but the inside stuff counting was exactly what we need to remain focused. His story also provided the powerful reminder of the importance of what we do and the difference we make in the lives of the patients. I have received tremendous feedback about Matt's presentation and know provided value to all that were in the room. It was especially relevant since the majority of our speakers focus on the technical side of healthcare engineering. It was refreshing to have a speaker focus more on personal development and as Matt says, 'human engineering.'"

—**Douglas Gish,** Minnesota Healthcare Engineer Association Conference Chair

"Matt Jones was fantastic way to kick off our annual AKMGMA Conference. He was so energetic and put out positive energy. The strategies shared to the managers will allow them to think out of the box and look at things in a different perspective. Matt kept our attendees engaged and his personal story is very inspirational. Attendees had such a positive comments about Matt on the survey, here is some of those comments: 'He is wonderful, recommend for next year, very dynamic speaker with lots of energy and great message, amazingly positive, practical, real, raw, honest, genuine, empowering, very positive and encouraging, great way to open a conference, it was fun to see contagion run throughout the other presentations-Victory!' Matt is very easy to work with, professional and so personable; he was completely prepared to get the audience fired up and ready to conquer the day!"

—**Linda Carroll,** Alaska Medical Group Management Association (AKMGMA)

"Matt Jones kicked off our conference in an unforgettable way, and attendees talked about him and his talk throughout the rest of the conference. His message was even more pertinent due to the challenges at the conference site. Our members were WOWED by Matt's story and how he related it to us. We feel that he went above and beyond in regards to communicating in a personal way to each attendee both before and after the talk. His effort of making a connection with everyone in the audience was truly astounding. Listening to Matt was a great reminder of the importance of our work. He made a lasting impact on our members and has our full recommendation as a speaker."

—**Stephen Slack,** Program Chair, Pennsylvania Association of Cancer Registrars

"Matt Jones exceeded all of our expectations with an inspiring story and an awesome keynote speech. He totally energized and motivated our attendees. The feedback was tremendous. The way he blended together humor, personal stories, and strategies related to our industry made a real impact. Matt has a real gift of connecting with his audience and raising the level of energy in a room. Our members were inspired, entertained, and left at the end of the day with key principles they can use in their everyday lives. We considered ourselves blessed to have Matt with us for our first AHMA CARH conference. I strongly recommend him as one of the best speakers in our 22-year history of CARH conferences and 16 year history of AHMA conferences."

—**Joseph B. Diehl,** Executive Director Washington State Council for Affordable and Rural Housing Affordable Housing Management Association of Washington

"Matt Jones provided a keynote for our winter conference that was out of this world. His closing keynote was one the highlights of a great conference. The way Matt held the attention of the audience at the end of a long day and dinner was amazing. At one point, you could hear a pin drop as the audience was captivated but his against all-odds-story of overcoming adversity. Then through the use of well-timed humor, the whole room was filled with laughter. Matt's talk was truly a gift as our industry has gone through some many changes. It was renewing and energizing in listening to him. He challenged, motivated, and encouraged us both personally and professionally. Matt is an amazing speaker and one of the best ones I have heard. If you are looking for a life-changing speaker whose message will entertain, inspire, and encourage, then Matt Jones is the speaker that you are looking for."

—**Susan H. Gerber,** Director Student Financial Services, Operations, Yale University

"Matt was a fantastic speaker. His presentation was fun, high-energy, inspirational, and drew from his real life experiences. He engaged our audience to help them "visualize their victory" in a constantly changing world. Matt overcame a tremendous travel obstacle to present at our convention, which demonstrated his drive to conquer his challenges. I was amazed he was able to make it through all the obstacles he faced in the 24 hours preceding his presentation. We were very pleased to have Matt share at our convention. He truly walks his talk. Matt Jones has my full recommendation and is an excellent choice for an inspirational speaker."

—**Theresa Rihanek. MHA, RHIA, CCS,** NHIMA Annual Convention Speaker Sub-Committee

"We were so thankful to be able to have Matt Jones as our speaker. He supercharged the room with an infusion of passion. Everyone in the room was moved by his exceptional talk and story that connected on a deep level. He is a captivating storyteller and speaker that brings out the champion spirit in others. Matt provided a fun and high-energy talk that was beneficial for all. The long line to get Matt's book and autograph was proof of the impact that he had on our group. He was the perfect speaker for the group and we were so fortunate to hear his words of inspiration."

—**Helen Cole, RN, MSN, OCN,** Unit Director, UPMC Cancer Centers

"Matt Jones is an exceptional and amazing speaker! Matt concluded our two-day state conference with an empowering, life-changing presentation. The conference participants left feeling positive, motivated and rejuvenated, which is difficult to do after listening to physicians talk about cancer for a day and a half. Matt is dedicated, compassionate and enthusiastic! No one could possibly walk away from one of Matt's talks without learning something or being inspired to do something. He shares strategies we can all use in our everyday life to stay focused and positive. He is an inspiration to all of us. He will be forever an inspiration to me! Matt, you were phenomenal! You by far exceeded by expectations! Thank you for sharing your experience with us. And letting us learn and grow from it."

—**Sara Biese, RHIT, CTR,** Fall Conference Host, Wisconsin Cancer Registrars Association

"Matt's ability to engage, excite, and enthuse the audience is amazing. His story is heartfelt and hits you hard…but through his challenges and ability to be resilient and rebound you are left saying if this young man can find the joy and treasure in life…why can't I? His personality and genuine nature is addictive and is applicable to all walks of people. Although, Mr. Jones is known for his battle with cancer and how his recovery changed his life, his talks are vibrant and interesting and keep his audiences enthralled. He invokes laughter while giving some of the best life lessons possible. All we can say is "Wow." He has touched our lives and we are sure he will impact yours as well. We recommend Matthew Jones to you without reservation. We hope you will give him the opportunity to address your industry."

—**Tanya Patterson-Stanley,** NYSFAAA Conference Co-Chair New York State Financial Aid Administrators Association

"We were very fortunate to have Matt Jones speak at our 14th Annual Leadership Conference. His inspirational, motivational, and interactive message on "Life's a Marathon" with 26.2 wining strategies for personal and professional success touched everyone who heard him. His time with our teams provided real life inspiration, along with everyday tools that can be used for greater success. Matt's energy and positive attitude are very contagious. Matt was instrumental in us delivering one of the "best" Leadership Conference in 14 years to over 500+ associates and vendors. I would highly recommend Matt as a speaker for any upcoming event."

—**Annie R. McClinton,** VP Training & Development Western National Group

"He engaged, energized and inspired our group. Our members were motivated and heard key strategies they can apply to their personal situations. Matt's story puts into perspective the challenges we all face and inspires people to become better individuals because of those challenges. We were uplifted by his enthusiasm and his story of perseverance and faith. Matt Jones experienced life-changing events, and he now carries a message that people need to hear. He is truly an inspiration and is a wonderful speaker."

—**Margaret L. Barnes,** President, Chapter 57 International Right of Way Association

"We were looking for a speaker that would not only inspire our managers but also provide practical strategies they could us at their properties. Matt fulfilled both wonderfully with a presentation that integrated our company's core values and made it feel like it was just for us. For two days from, Keynote to interactive training, the stories, lessons, and principles he shared made a lasting impact."

—**Lee Schwendiman,** Dei Communities, Vice President, Revenue Management

"He inspired, wowed, and transformed the over 500 of our members in attendance. His story was a great example for our members to follow when faced with daily challenges. He kept the whole audience energized, entertained, and educated throughout his whole talk. The feedback on his presentation was phenomenal and the attendees referred back to it throughout the rest of the conference. I recommend Matt as a speaker for your group. He has a unique ability to fire up, pump up, and inspire audiences."

—**Kathy Roberson,** President, Mississippi Association of School Business Officials (MASBO)

"Terrific! His presentation was a homerun performance. He provided a full hour's worth of energy-packed entertainment, encouragement, and education. I received nothing but praise about Matt's inspiring talk. He provided a first class presentation and his enthusiasm and energy is contagious. His personal story of perseverance was a great reminder to our members of what it takes to be successful. The strategies Matt shared contained lifelong value that can be put into practice immediately. He was a real asset to our conference and I highly recommend him as a speaker."

—**Marie T. Mercer,** Virginia Executive Director, National Association of Insurance and Financial Advisors

MOTIVATE AND INSPIRE OTHERS!

"SHARE THIS BOOK"

Retail $24.95

Special Quantity Discounts

5-20 BOOKS	$21.95
21-99 BOOKS	$18.95
100-499 BOOKS	$15.95
500-999 BOOKS	$10.95
1,000+ BOOKS	$8.95

To Place an Order Contact:

(213) 291-9873

Matt@MatthewDJones.com

www.MatthewDJones.com

THE IDEAL PROFESSIONAL SPEAKER FOR YOUR NEXT EVENT!

Any organization, association, or business that wants to inspire their members or employees to become "extraordinary," needs to hire Matt for a keynote

TO CONTACT OR BOOK MATT TO SPEAK:

Matt Jones International, Inc.

13492 Research Blvd, Suite 120, #186

Austin, TX 78750

1-800-676-1598

Matt@MatthewDJones.com

www.MatthewDJones.com

5 Reasons Why Meeting Planners and Event Coordinators Like You Love to Book Matt Jones:

1. Matt has a Life-Changing Story

Your attendees will discover a greater potential inside them through hearing Matt's remarkable story of going from being a 3x Cancer Conqueror, to relearning how walk, to running marathons around the world.

2. Matt is an Inspiring Speaker

Your attendees will be captivated by Matt's mix of emotion, humor, and storytelling. They will walk away after Matt's talk hearing an unforgettable message shared from the heart.

3. Matt has a Life-Transforming Message

Following the strategies Matt presents, your attendee's lives are guaranteed to be changed forever as Matt has the unique ability to bring out the best in individuals and organizations.

4. Matt Shares Time-Tested Strategies for Success

Your attendees will experience positive results both personally and professionally. His strategies have been time-tested and proven through his "against-all-odds" life inspiring story, and backed up through research in the field of psychology, along with results achieved by his audiences.

5. Matt Provides Value

You get the following when you book Matt:

Valuable Information *(Your group will receive information new information with a guarantee to provide lasting value)*

Action Steps *(Practical ideas that your attendees can you immediately for improved results)*

Lasting Impact *(Matt's presentation focuses on results that last a lifetime for your attendees)*

Useful Strategies and Solutions *(Guaranteed to be relevant to the challenges, needs, and goals of your group)*

Easy to Work With *(Matt will be the easiest speaker you have ever had to work with)*

TABLE OF CONTENTS

DEDICATION

This book is dedicated to my amazing family and special friends who have shown me what true love is. I am so blessed and thankful for all that you have done for me. I love you all so much. Thank you for being so wonderful and making such a profound difference in my life.

Judy Jones (Mom)

Bob Jones (Dad)

Joanna Jones (Sister)

Jennifer Jones (Sister)

Tim Washburn (Donor)

Jordan Crow (Best friend)

Foreword

You can feel it in his presence. You can see it in his eyes. Though he appears to be very youthful, Matt Jones is an old soul in a young body.

I will never forget the first time I saw him stand before an audience, balance himself, square his shoulders and tell his story about being diagnosed with leukemia. Just as he was getting ready to take life by the horns he had a less than ten percent chance of survival.

The room was silent, eyes were teary and hearts were touched. Every life was changed by his example of faith, courage and the power of love.

Cancer is a formidable foe. I know. I was diagnosed with it myself, and it took everything in me to fight it. It's an enemy no one wants to encounter, but if you do, it helps to be equipped with more than what comes out of a doctor's mouth.

Matt Jones shares the intimate details of his own struggle with cancer. Diagnosed at 23, just as he was beginning to think about a future, just as he was beginning to outline a path, he was faced with a brick wall.

Matt uses his courageous battle with cancer as a powerful backdrop to tap into your faith and personal power in order to beat the odds. But this book isn't just about facing cancer. It's about facing whatever obstacles life throws at you. Your obstacle may be a job loss. Or it may be whatever you think your worst nightmare is.

Matt gives powerful keys that helped him move from tragedy to triumph. These are the intangible tools that can give you an edge. I know the principles he discusses can make a difference in your life. A positive attitude, for instance, isn't just about a smile. It's about choosing to believe you will beat the thing that wants to beat you. It's about refusing to let negativity and worry, make you feel even worse. Many people doubt the power of the mind, but I know, just as Matt knows, the mind is a powerful weapon that most people do not use to their advantage.

Matt also recognized something important; often our hard times make us better people. Matt came out of his cancer experience a stronger and more powerful person. He became more driven, more empowered, and indeed, more in touch with his spiritual nature.

How do you meet your hard times? How do you meet your struggles? Do you look at them with fear and anxiety, anger and dread? Or do you accept them as another opportunity to demonstrate your faith? How you meet your challenge very often will determine how you beat your challenge.

If you are looking for a way to face your fight with whatever obstacle your encounter, this is the book for you. It can help you through your dark days and enable you to create a bright future.

I've used these same tools, and I can say it with conviction: They work if you work them.

-Les Brown
"The World's Leading Motivational Speaker,"
Recipient of the National Speakers Association's CPAE Speaker Hall of Fame Award (NSA's highest award for speaking excellence)

Introduction

"I am convinced that many times, in the course of our lives, God challenges us with a golden opportunity, a seemingly impossible hurdle, or a terrible tragedy . . . and how we react - or fail to react - determines the course of our future."

—**Og Mandino,** A Better Way to Live

Imagine being twenty-five years old, and not able to tie your own shoes. Trying to read, but the paragraphs are a shaky jumble of words you can't decipher. Searching for words to speak, but they don't seem to come out right.

Just a while earlier, your most pressing concern was graduating college. And now, here you are, laid up in a hospital bed, and fighting your biggest battle: cancer. Even though I share my story in this book, it isn't about me and it's not about my battle. It's about sharing with you the choices I made to get me through a life-changing event; the choices that helped me recover from a devastating diagnosis, and the proven strategies I and countless others have used to face any number of trying times of adversity so you can use them in your life.

This book is about inspiring you to overcome adversity, big or small, and achieve greater victory in your life. My intention in writing this is to help you reach your true purpose and potential, even in the face of seemingly hard times. This book is about giving you real hope to make it to the other side of the challenges you face.

You have gone through and will go through more challenges, or as I like to call them, "character building experiences." It's called life. It can be easy to falter, get discouraged, and become overwhelmed by those tiring situations; allowing them to beat you down. But that doesn't have to be the case. Whether you're facing the end to what you thought was a forever relationship, lost your job, or your dealing with a health challenge, your life is not over!

No matter how great the adversity you're facing may seem, with a few simple choices, you can get through them, and grow because of them. I know because that is what happened to me.

Life can be difficult at times, yet ultimately, it's overwhelmingly good. You're meant to live a life of health, wealth, and abundance. Your tragedies, hardships, and challenges can be turned into triumph; something positive can come out of any negative situation, even the one you're facing right now. Perhaps it's the hard times that become part of living your purpose. I know that was my case with cancer.

If I hadn't gone through the battle with cancer, I might never have known the conqueror inside of me waiting to surface. Perhaps I wouldn't have realized the resolve that comes from struggle, or the certainty of purpose that comes from looking at the possibility of something that threatens your very existence.

When I got the phone call from my doctor numbing me and shattering my happy-go-lucky life, I couldn't have known that the journey I was about to go on would be a blessing to myself and so many others.

Each of your hard times polishes you, stretching you to become the person that sometimes you aren't even aware you can become. You become a better version of yourself; bringing out the best you there is. This is what happened to me. Your "character building experiences" teach you something about yourself.

At times it's no fun to endure, but when you look back, you see how they helped to shape and mold you. Your hard times often become the building blocks to your greatest successes. Out of your darkest nights come your brightest days.

Part of the lesson that comes from going through adversity is reaching your true potential. Your life challenges help you become, as the once used United States Army recruiting slogan said, "Be all that you can be."

Your true potential is the power and possibilities that live within you right now, waiting to be developed and brought to the forefront.

Your true potential is what psychologist Dr. Abraham Maslow called "Self-Actualization." It's described as the yearning for becoming what you are capable of being. It's the intense and burning desire, the driving need, for you to be and do that which you were born to do. Through my experiences I learned that out of your mess comes your message; out of your test comes your testimony. No matter the amount of success, happiness, and fulfillment you've had up to this point, it's only the beginning of the beginning of what you are capable of doing. You have just begun to scratch the surface of what is possible for your life.

In this book you will discover how to transcend adversity and experience greater victory in all areas of your life. When it comes to overcoming adversity and achieving greater victory, it's not the outside stuff that matters, but the inside stuff that counts.

I call that inside stuff your "Marathon Mentality," which is the mindset to push through the walls of negativity, setbacks, and obstacles, to cross your finish line and achieve greater victory.

You develop your "Marathon Mentality" by making three choices:

1. **The choice to "Visualize Your Victory"**
2. **The choice to "Take Action"**
3. **The choice to "Elevate Your Attitude"**

This book will help you move toward developing your "Marathon Mentality." I have confidence that if you make these three choices I discovered from going through my adversity, you will be able live out your true potential. You will be able to face hardships and not let them defeat you. You will be able to attain career and personal satisfaction along with success. You will be able to achieve greater victory. I know you will be able to do this, because against all odds I've been able to do it.

Just as I was able to overcome my "character building experience" with cancer and have gone on to live a life of contribution, so can you. Your personal challenge may not be cancer, but that doesn't make it any less significant. This book is proof that no matter how insurmountable an obstacle may seem it can be overcome! I hope my story will serve as an inspiration that anything is possible, that it will be your guide in this wonderful adventure called life.

This book, quite simply, is for you! It's written to help inspire you to discover and become the very best you possible. You have a special and unique purpose; you have talents and abilities that no one else possesses. Your purpose is related to those talents and abilities. One of the reasons I share my story is to empower others like you to overcome their trials and tribulations in order to experience greater victory; this is part of my unique and special purpose.

Due to the personal nature of my story, some of the names that appear have been changed. Always remember, you have a special purpose and only you can fulfill it. As I share my story, remember it's also your story!

CHOICE ONE

VISUALIZE YOUR VICTORY

"If you can see it, and believe it's possible, you can do it."

CHAPTER 1:
Perception is Reality

September 11, 2002 is a day I will never forget. It was the worst and best day of my life. Each of us has turning points; times when your destiny intersects with fate and your life is forever changed in unexpected ways. This may have been when you met your significant other, the birth of your child, or when the very fiber of your being was tested.

Welcome sign to my hometown of Emporia, Kansas.

For me, it was, hearing three words from a phone call. It was the fall semester of my senior year in college at Emporia State University, a small school of about 5,500 students located in my hometown of Emporia, Kansas: a small Midwest town with a population of just over 24,000, when school is in session. A lot of people don't realize it's the founding city of Veteran's Day and the birthplace of the legendary basketball coach for the North Carolina Tar Heels, Dean Smith. I was a small-town boy with big city dreams.

My hero was Arnold Schwarzenegger and I wanted to be a competitive bodybuilder. My plan after graduation was to move to California and continue to get pumped up, become a personal trainer to the stars, and have my own infomercial. As you know, your life doesn't always turn out as you plan.

As I began my fall semester, I was excited to start my new workout program; my goal was to attain 235 pounds of rock-solid muscle. The previous summer I became a certified personal trainer by The American

College of Sports Medicine, which is the gold standard of certification. Everything was aligning; my intense effort and dedication were about to pay off. But, within seconds, all of that would change, upon hearing three words you never want to hear.

VICTORY THROUGH CHALLENGES

The one thing you and I have in common is that we both have gone through challenges. Maybe your challenge has been greater than mine or maybe less. Either way, what is more important than the reality of the challenge you have faced, currently facing, or will face is your perception of it. It's not what happens to you, it's how you see it. Life isn't about your circumstances; it's about your choices. If you choose, your hard times can become a catalyst for growth. They can catapult you to success beyond your wildest dreams. It's through your darkest nights that cause your brightest days appear. This would be one of the most important lessons I learned.

Once again I like to call challenges "character building experiences," because character is forged through the fires of adversity.

Life couldn't be better; the leaves were just beginning to change color and the crisp smell of autumn was in the air. I was so excited for this semester.

The dream of becoming the next Arnold gripped my mind as I was preparing to take my body to new heights. I was pumped, rearing to go, and ready to crush it in the weight room. You can imagine

That summer had been one of the best times of my life; the fall would become one of my worst.

the shock I felt when I couldn't even finish my first workout. At the time I figured it was due to the intensity; never in my worst nightmare did I think that workout would be the last in my pursuit of becoming a professional bodybuilder.

Picture from my first photo shot as an aspiring bodybuilder.

The next day was the first day of school. I was so tired that I missed every morning class, barely making it to my afternoon one. My body was completely drained; it felt as though I hadn't slept in weeks. I barely had enough energy to get out of bed! I began sleeping up to sixteen hours a day and was still totally exhausted; just walking up stairs caused a shortness of breath.

A few days before, I was doing intense workouts. My mind was reeling. How could I go from doing leg presses with over seven hundred pounds to not even being able to walk up two flights of stairs? Then, other strange things began happening. My throat became swollen. I would cut myself shaving and couldn't get the bleeding to stop. One of my good friends, Jordan, commented that I was the worst shaver ever, because I always had tissue on my face to get the bleeding to stop. My gums became red, swollen, and sunken down; I bled just brushing my teeth. I continued missing my classes.

At one point I wondered to myself, "What's happening to me? Asking the question, "Am I dying?"

Mono had been making its rounds through campus and several of my friends had come down with it, so I figured that's what I had; in two or three months I would be back to my old self, throwing weights around the gym like they were rag-dolls. I scheduled an appointment with my family doctor to get a note for my professors since I was missing so many classes. The appointment was for September 11, 2002.

The Sunday before, I had planned to watch the opening kickoff of football, but instead I spent the whole day in bed, completely exhausted. It was one of the worst days of my life and it would only get worse. I remember having just enough strength to get up and go get a bacon cheeseburger, fries, and a chocolate Frosty at Wendy's. During that twenty-four hour period I slept twenty-three hours!

You can imagine how frustrated I was with being sick, how I just wanted to be back to my old self, sweating in the gym and pumping iron. At my doctor's appointment I shared my symptoms and he agreed that most likely I had mono. They did some tests and I anxiously waited for the results, which came back negative for mono.

I received a doctor's note for my professors saying I had mono-like symptoms, and my blood was sent to a lab for more tests. He told me that if I didn't get better to come back in a couple of weeks because it could be something more.

I didn't think any more about it until a little after one o'clock, when my phone rang. I had no idea when I answered it that my life would change forever.

The one constant in life is change. Many times the changes you experience are subtle, but every once in a while, you experience change of a seismic proportion. It's in these moments that your life is altered forever. They can either transform or destroy you; the choice is yours.

"Hello, this is Matt."

"Matt, this is Dr. McNamara."

When the doctor calls you at home it's not a good sign!

"Yes, how can I help you?" I nervously asked, curious why my doctor was calling me.

> I thought to myself, "The reason I had more white blood cells than the average person was because I had more muscles."

"Matt, we have some good news and some bad. You're sicker than we thought. Your white blood cell count is five times greater than normal."

"Isn't that a good thing, since they fight infection?" I replied.

"Matt, you do not understand; they're abnormal."

Confused I asked, "What does that mean?"

"It's a red flag for leukemia, you have cancer."

In that moment, it was as if someone reached down and pushed the pause button on my life. I was instantly in a state of shock and disbelief; I could barely breathe. I couldn't even process the words I was hearing.

"Cancer . . . me? How could this be?" I was a certified personal trainer, always working out, and I prided myself in eating healthy food. This isn't supposed to happen to someone in his or her early twenties. "Maybe other people, but not me," I thought.

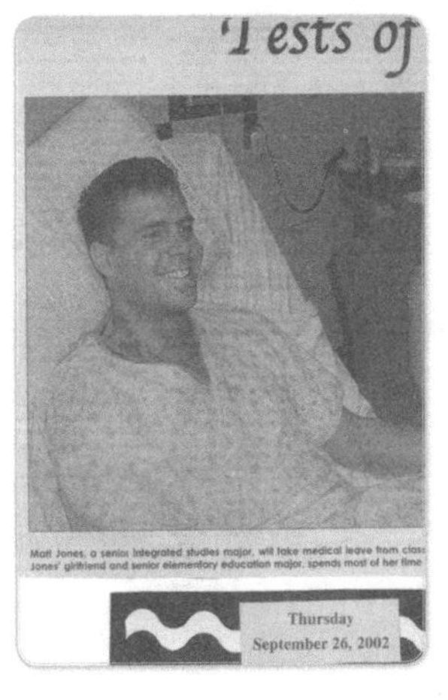

Picture from my first week in the hospital at St. Francis in Topeka, Kansas.

Interrupting my thought pattern were the words, "Matt you need to go to St. Francis Hospital in Topeka to begin treatment right away."

Leukemia is the leading cause of cancer death among men under the age of forty. I was diagnosed with acute myeloid leukemia or AML, which is a rapidly progressing blood cancer that results in the accumulation of immature, functionless cells in the marrow and blood. Dr. McNamara wanted me to immediately check into the hospital because survival depends on getting treatment as soon as possible.

Without treatment, Acute Myeloid Leukemia becomes fatal within a few weeks to months.

One of the things I'm most grateful for was that Dr. McNamara didn't stop with just the bad news.

"Matt, the good news is that you can beat this. It's not going to be easy, but you can do it."

The good news is that you can also beat the challenges in your life.

There is a Jewish proverb that says, "There is life and death in the power of the tongue." Dr. McNamera planted a seed of life within me. No matter the adversity you're facing, you can get through it!

VISUALIZE YOUR VICTORY

The first choice you must make to develop your "Marathon Mentality" in order to achieve greater victory and overcome adversity is to "Visualize Your Victory." One of the examples I share in my keynotes is what you're taught to do when you spin out of control at racecar driving school.

You're taught not to focus on the wall, but instead where you want to go on the track. The reason is that where you place your focus is where you'll end up.

This is a great metaphor for life. Unfortunately, too many people focus on what they don't want. They talk about the weather being too hot or cold, their knee or back that hurts, or the latest things that so and so did to them.

"Where your attention goes, your energy flows, and your results show."
–T Harv Eker

What are you focusing on? Where is your attention directed? The important thing to remember is to focus your attention on where you want to go.

Visualizing your victory is about getting clarity and developing laser-like focus. Perhaps you were like me as a child, and used a magnifying glass to start small fires with the concentration of the sun's rays. Similarly, to overcome adversity, you have to have the same concentration. Think, talk, and plan on what you want versus focusing on what you don't want.

Upon hearing the words from Dr. McNamara, my first reaction was to focus on the cancer. I repeated the words, "You have cancer" over and over again. My turning point came in realizing in that particular moment I couldn't change the circumstance of being diagnosed, yet I could choose where to place my focus. I made the constant decision to allow the doctors to focus on what they do best, treating the cancer. For me, I had to focus not on the outside circumstances but on my inner mindset.

This switch in mindset was one of the biggest factors in conquering cancer. I made the choice to Visualize My Victory.

Realizing that perception is reality allows you to make the choice to "Visualize Your Victory," even if you're in the midst of the flames of adversity. It allows you to recognize that your life is not determined by your circumstances, but rather your perception of them.

Below is a picture of glass of water. In my keynotes I ask the audience the age-old questions, "Is the glass half full, or half empty?" How would you answer that question?

"Is this glass half full or half empty?

After asking that question to my audience, the optimist in the room answer the glass is half full and the realists answer that the glass is half empty. Then I share that the glass is actually one hundred percent full. Fifty percent of the glass is filled with water and the other fifty percent is filled with air. It's not your circumstances that determine your life or even reality, but your perception and the meaning you give those circumstances.

WHAT YOU FOCUS ON EXPANDS

One of the most important lessons I learned in my victory over cancer is realizing that what you focus on is what you get back. This is why when people leave my talk I want them remembering the word **VICTORY**. One of the ways we learn is kinesthetically, which involves moving your body; so to engage the audience and help them to remember the word **VICTORY**, I have them do a victory pose by raising their arms above their heads and shout, "**VICTORY!**"

An added benefit of the victory pose comes from research done by by social psychologist Amy Cuddy. Her research shows that you can change your life by changing your body language. She stated that one of the most universal body language poses is the victory pose; it's a universal sign of empowerment, strength, and achievement. It transcends cultures and can be seen around the world from the ancient Greeks in the Olympics to present day sports fans after their favorite team scores a goal. Researchers have even found that people blind since birth will do the victory pose after accomplishing an achievement.

I recommend you do it right know; raise your arms above your head in a "V" shape and shout "VICTORY!" Doing the victory pose will put you in a peak state of empowerment.

Doing so creates an anchor, so you'll remember it long after reading this book or hearing me speak. Proof of this happened one time in Michigan where I was eating at an airport restaurant before a flight and I heard someone sitting next to me shout out, "Hey brother, Victory!" At first I was bewildered hearing someone shout those words, but then he said he saw me speak at a conference.

My experience with cancer helped me realize that every day you wake up is a victory! Several years ago, I was the closing speaker for a sales group in New York. The next morning I was the keynote speaker for a healthcare group in Portland, Oregon. My connecting flight was at

Chicago O'Hare. If you've ever had to fly out of there you know it can be a "character building experience."

My favorite part of my talk is celebrating the victories of the audience by crossing the finish line together and shouting "VICTORY, VICTORY, VICTORY!"

My connecting flight at O'Hare was the last one out that night and I spoke at eight o'clock the next morning. If I missed my flight I would miss my talk! Of course, my flight to Chicago was delayed. After we finally landed in Chicago we got stuck on the tarmac. By the time we reached the gate my flight was due to take off in ten minutes! Being optimistic, I just knew that our arrival gate would be next to the departure gate. No such luck, instead we were in a totally separate terminal.

One of my favorite things about being a professional speaker is the privilege to travel around the world.

While waiting to deplane, I called the airline to see if there were any other flights with another airline. There were none; if I didn't catch my flight then I'd have to take one in the morning, which meant missing my talk! I told the airplane representative I had to make my plane and asked for her advice. She said, "Run, Forrest, run!" As soon as I got off the plane I made a mad rush down the jet way trying to conjure up my inner Forrest Gump.

Imagine running through the airport trying to catch your plane that's one terminal away (which in O'Hare is close to the distance of a marathon). You're huffing and puffing as sweat is coming down your forehead; you're weaving in and out of people on your left and right and dodging people in front of you to avoid a collision. The bag you're carrying in your right arm gets so heavy that you switch it to your left hand side.

As you're running, out of the corner of your eye, you see a sign for the two hundred and eight million dollar Powerball jackpot. Think how nice it would be to win the two hundred and eight million dollar Powerball jackpot! I have an important question for you: if you could win the two hundred and eight million dollar Powerball jackpot or wake up tomorrow morning, which would you choose? It's a no brainer!

Imaging waking up tomorrow and having $86,400 credited to your bank account. The catch, it does not carry over and at the end of the day, you lose everything you did not spend. This happens every single day. It gets even better! Every single day you are given 86,400 seconds, at the end of the day they are gone forever. How will you spend your 86,400 seconds each day? If you would please, take a big deep breath in and breathe out. How big of a check would you write for that? Every day you wake up and every breath in and out is a victory. Once again, what you focus on in life is what you get. As a side note, I was able to make my flight! Victory!

WHAT'S YOUR COMPELLING VISION?

There is a timeless truth that says, "Where there is no vision the people perish." What vision do you have for your life? Most people go through life aimless, without a vision. They're like a leaf on a windy day, blown about by the wind. Webster's dictionary defines vision as, "An object of imagination." You can create your reality by the imagination of your mind.

What Vision Are You Visualizing?

What do you want to do, be, and have in your life? You have to be able to see your vision in your mind's eye. Your vision is your victory. From that comes your special purpose. It's the reason why you're here on this earth.

Right now I would like you to look on the inside of your index finger. What do you call those lines you see? Of course, it's your fingerprint, which is uniquely yours. No one has ever had it, currently has it, or will ever have it. Just like you have a unique and special fingerprint, you have a unique and special purpose in life!

You've been given a special gift that no one presently alive, who has lived in the past, or who will live in the future can match. Just like your fingerprints and DNA, you have a special talent. This talent is unique to you and becomes a gift to humanity when fully expressed. Michelangelo had the gift of art, Shakespeare of writing, and Beethoven of music. You also have something special to give.

Unfortunately, many people go to their graves never having used their talents. Do you have a book inside of you, a song, or your own business that you could start? It's never too late and never too soon to play the music given to you.

Grandma Moses was in her late seventies when she started to paint. After turning one hundred, she painted over two hundred paintings. Some of her work is on display at the Smithsonian. Mozart was only five when he wrote his first composition.

Dr. Myles Munroe said, "The wealthiest places in the world are not gold mines, oil fields, diamond mines or banks. The wealthiest place is the cemetery. There lies companies that were never started, masterpieces that were never painted. In the cemetery there is buried the greatest treasure of untapped potential. There is a treasure within you that must come out. Don't go to the grave with your treasure still within YOU."

You have a special purpose!

You're significant! Just think how impossible the odds are to even be born! The adversity you had to overcome just to be conceived. One sperm out of hundreds of millions of other sperm had to survive and find an egg for the process of conception to occur. It's miraculous! You had to survive to the first trimester, then the second, after that the third, and then finally, the act of birth.

WOW! You'll never face those odds again! When you recognize how remarkable it is to even show up in this life, you begin to realize you're no accident! You were meant to be here, which means you have a reason for being here. This brings us to your purpose. You are worthy of your purpose. Life is the fact that you showed up; your special purpose is the reason that you showed up.

Life, at times, can seem unfair; you get knocked down. Sometimes life throws a great obstacle in your way. As I tried to process the words from Dr. McNamara, it felt as if life was hitting me upside the head with a two-by-four. As I hung up the phone, I was numb, and my carefree existence shattered like a vase falling upon a tile floor. I was in disbelief, scared, and bewildered. I couldn't have known then that the journey I'd go on would become a blessing to me as well as so many others.

I experienced every emotion a human being could have over the course of my battle from diagnosis, to treatment, to remission, to relapse, and back again. As I look back on what I've been through, I can tell you with one hundred percent certainty that having cancer is directly related to my life's purpose. From that "character building experience," I'm able to share with others and inspire them to live better lives. The same is true for you and "character building experiences" you have gone through and you will go through.

I learned so much lying flat on my back. What about you? What hard time has served to make you a stronger, better person? Looking back on it, cancer, though quite unwelcome, gave my life greater meaning. I hoped my battle with it would be a sprint; instead, it was a marathon.

I had no idea how difficult the journey ahead would be; had I known then, I'm not sure I could've done it. When making the choice to "Visualize Your Victory," you have to see it and believe it's possible before you can do it.

VICTORY THROUGH PERSONAL MASTERY

One way you build belief in the victory you're visualizing is through personal mastery. This is the practice of developing yourself through personal development. Even though I didn't realize it at the time, this concept was introduced to me as a small child thanks to a garden and a gopher.

I come from a line of farmers on both sides of my family. At five years old I figured I was destined to become a farmer; my grandfather had been one and when he retired his hobby became gardening. I was so excited when he asked me if I wanted to plant a garden; my destiny of becoming a farmer was coming true.

We went to the hardware store and picked up packets of seeds: radishes, carrots, and one more, for the life of me I can't remember what it was. My mom got me some bib overalls and a straw hat. I was now officially a farmer. The first thing I remember is that my grandfather and I dug holes, then we placed the seeds, put fertilizer in the hole and filled it in with dirt. Then my grandfather said, “Matt, make sure you water your crops and pull the weeds every day.”

The number one thing you can do to improve yourself professionally is to improve yourself personally.

All summer long I eagerly ran outside each day to water my crops and pull the weeds, always wearing my bib overalls and straw hat. Finally, it was harvest time; I was so excited I could hardly sleep. It was like the night before Christmas! I was so enthusiastic and motivated that I was going to have vegetables for breakfast. My dream of becoming a farmer had come true. Then, I met the cousin of the gopher in the movie *Caddyshack*. Upon reaching my garden, I saw him eating the last of my vegetables; the garden had become a buffet for the gopher. My little heart was crushed, and that was the end of my farming career.

I share this story because your mind, like a garden, needs to be watered with positivity on a daily basis. You must also pull out the weeds of negativity daily. In addition to what I learned from my grandfather, I discovered you have to watch out for gophers; they are the people, places, and things that will rob you of your victory seeds and crops that you’ve planted.

It’s your mindset that determines your perception of your reality. The investment in time, energy, and money into my own self-development and mastery allowed me to hold the perception of a greater victory coming from my reality of having cancer.

You can only get out of your refrigerator what you put in; the same is true for your mind.

F.L.O.S.S. YOUR MIND

During my talks, when I am speaking about personal mastery, I like to share the metaphor of flossing, which is one of the most, if not the most important thing you can do for your teeth. Just like you need to floss daily, you also need to "FLOSS" your mind daily to get rid of the buildup of "negativity plaque."

Using each letter of the word "FLOSS," I'd like to give you five simple and easy ways to "FLOSS" your mind on a daily basis.

Find the Blessing
Listen
Open to Learning
Start and End the Day Reading
Say Affirmations

FIND THE BLESSING

The first way to floss your mind is to *find the blessing*. Every day when you wake up, start by thinking of three blessings. You should write them down in a notepad or journal you keep by your bedside. They can be as simple as the fact that you woke up, which considering the alternative is a very big blessing! Some others include being thankful for the roof over your head, the bed you slept in, and the opportunity to experience another day!

Another is when you wake up and have a job (service) to go to. The key is to write them down; research has shown it's more effective. This mental floss activity focuses your mind on what's good in your life, putting you in a peak state, and allowing you to be solution oriented throughout the day.

One of the greatest blessings of sharing my story and message is helping others develop themselves personally and professionally.

Remember, what you focus on is what you get back. Do this for a few weeks or months, and then look back on all the blessings which are the victories in your life. I wish I would've known about this while going through my adventure with cancer.

To demonstrate how simple and easy this is, below are three places to write down three blessings in your life:

Blessing Number One:

____

Blessing Number Two:

____

Blessing Number Three:

____

I also recommend making this the first thing you do at work (play), because you're putting yourself in a peak frame of mind for the day.

LISTEN

The second way to mentally floss daily and remove "negativity plaque" is to *listen*. Just like a refrigerator, you can only get out of it what you put in it. As one of my all-time favorite motivational speakers, Keith Harrell said, "You have to monitor your ear gate." One of the easiest ways to floss your mind is by listening to "Automobile University," which is listening to educational, empowering, and instructional audio programs while in your automobile. Make your drive time your victory time. The average American spends up to five hundred hours a year in their vehicle.

It's a great opportunity while driving to work, the grocery store, or picking up your children from school, to feed your mind inspirational, motivational, and educational audio programs. Just think, with five hundred hours over the course of a year, you could even learn a new language. A great resource to find audio programs is Nightingale-Conant located at www.nightingale.com.

It's also important to make time for inner listening. One way you gain clarity is by listening to your inner voice. At times our inner voice can be drowned out by the constant noise we experience. Think for a moment, 'When was the last time you experienced complete silence?"

Most people are uncomfortable with silence. A friend of mine always turns on the television immediately when entering a hotel room to rid it of the quietness. Another common thing you see today is people continually occupied with their phone. One thing I recommend is creating quiet times in your day. This can be as simple as turning off your car stereo or giving yourself a break from the data-sphere that so many people are addicted to.

OPEN TO LEARNING

The third daily mental floss activity is open to learning. The fact that you're reading this proves you're *open to learning*. One of my goals when

I read a book, listen to an audio program, attend a seminar, or listen to a speaker, is to learn one new thing or be reminded of something I already knew. If I can learn just one new thing, or be reminded of one thing, it was worth my whole investment of time and money.

I read a great story about the founder of the martial arts school of Kung Fu; he was about to pass away and he instructed his students to bury him in a white belt. This confused them since a white belt was for beginners. However, the master wanted his students to realize that you're never done learning and you should always consider yourself a student. In this "information overload society" we live in, it's essential to become a lifelong learner.

START AND END THE DAY READING

The fourth way to remove the "negativity plaque" from your mind is to *start and end the day reading*. The dynamic motivational speaker Charlie "Tremendous" Jones said, "You will be the same person you are today five years from now except for two things; the people you meet and the books you read."

Did you know that the average person reads less than one nonfiction book a year and according to *The World Almanac* watches over thirty hours of television a week? You think about it, that's like having an unpaid part-time job! I want to commend you for reading this book; it proves you're above average!

The good news is that a study featured in *USA Today*, found that three minutes of reading a day makes a difference. It is not about the amount your read, it's rather or not you apply it. An example from my life is how one quote from one book provided my victory to visualize while battling cancer. In an upcoming chapter, I will share that quote with you. Just think what might have happened to me if instead of taking a few minutes to read the book with that quote, I'd been watching TV.

At my talks I give out victory quote cards, containing some of the quotes I share when speaking. I recommend that audience members tape them to their computer at work so they can start and end their workday reading inspirational quotes. I also encourage them to take as many as they'd like and give them to co-workers, friends, family, and especially to the naysayers in their lives.

SAY AFFIRMATIONS

The final way to mentally floss is to *say affirmations*. One of the biggest challenges I faced in my adversity with cancer was the negative inner dialogue; I had to replace it with life affirming positive statements. One of my favorite affirmations to say is, "I'm too blessed to be stressed." If someone cuts me off in traffic, I repeat, "I'm too blessed to be stressed." If my flight is delayed I think over and over, "I'm too blessed to be stressed!"

Read Daily to Fire Up, Pump Up, and Inspire Yourself

"Visualize your Victory, Take Action, and Check your Attitude."

"If you can see it, believe it's possible, you can do it."

"It's not the outside stuff that matters, but the inside stuff that counts."

"Character is forged through the fires of adversity."

Matt Jones International

MATT JONES • The Ideal Professional Speaker for Your Next Event!
www.MatthewDJones.com • Matt@MatthewDJones.com • 800-676-1598

It would be my pleasure to send you Victory cards as a free gift to you. Email me at www.MatthewDJones.com with your mailing address and how many you'd like.

I'd like to share with you some powerful resources when it comes to affirmations. The first is a set of affirmations by author Christian Larson.

I've adapted them into the first person and have provided them below for you:

Victory Affirmations

- I am so strong that nothing can disturb my peace of mind.
- I talk health, happiness, and prosperity to every person I meet.
- I make all my friends feel that there is something worthwhile in them.
- I look at the sunny side of everything and make my optimism come true.
- I think only of the best, I work only for the best and I experience only the best.
- I am just as enthusiastic about the success of others as I am about my own.
- I forget the mistakes of the past and press on to the greater achievements of the future.
- I wear a cheerful expression at all times and give a smile to every living creature I meet.
- I give so much time to improving myself that I have no time to criticize others.
- I am too large for worry, too noble for anger, too strong for fear, and too happy to permit the presence of trouble.
- I think well of myself and I proclaim this fact to the world, not in loud word, but in great deeds.
- I live in the faith that the whole world is on my side, so long as I am true to the best that is in me.

—Adapted from Christian Larson

A second resource I'd like to give you is my adaptation from Keith Harrell's book, *Attitude Is Everything*. You can use the template below to create your personal victory affirmation to read each day. It's a great way to start your day and remind yourself throughout of how special, wonderful, and powerful you are.

Personal Victory Affirmation

I ________________________________, am victorious! I have a unique and special purpose. There has never been, and there will never be, anyone like me. I am an original. I am a one-of-a-kind person who possesses special talents and gifts that bring value to the world. I was born to bless others. I was born to achieve great victory. I have what it takes to experience victory in my life.

I am victorious.

I am solution oriented.

I speak words of life.

I am full of positive energy.

I am the master of my own destiny.

I am too blessed too be stressed.

I help others to achieve victory.

I am happy.

I am full of love.

I am full of peace.

By being blessed with all of my unique talents, all things are possible for me, when I believe. Today is my day to experience victory for myself and for others.

________________________________, go out and have a Victorious Day!

Besides saying affirmations, it's also powerful to listen to them. One of the things you can do is to record the previous personal affirmations in your own voice and listen to yourself affirming your victory on a daily basis. A second powerful thing you can do is to make an investment in affirmation albums and listen to them daily, perhaps in your automobile?

In order to make the choice to "Visualize Your Victory" you must realize that perception is reality. It's not what happens to you that matters but your perception and the meaning you give the event.

By making the choice to visualize my victory I discovered that the reality of getting cancer was not a curse, but a blessing.

CHAPTER 2:
Believe It's Possible

When I got off the phone after hearing those three life-altering words from Dr. McNamara, I turned towards my girlfriend at the time, Ashley, who was sitting on my bed. I didn't want to tell her. I didn't want to tell anyone. I didn't want to acknowledge it. Yet, she could see by the look on my face and hear in the tone of the conversation that something was extremely wrong.

She said, "Matt, who was that, what's wrong?"

I just looked at her, trying to say those three horrible words. I was frozen in place, frozen in time. I mouthed the words, but nothing came out. It felt like an eternity before those three words came out. I started by saying, "That was my doctor; he said that my white blood cell count is five times greater than normal . . . I have cancer . . . it's leukemia." We stood there in silence, trying to process the news.

I could see the confused look in her eyes. Tears rolled down our faces as I told her I had to go to St. Francis right away to start treatment. Those words were the most difficult I've ever spoken. To this day it's all so surreal, like a nightmare you desperately hope to wake up from. In a span of seconds my life forever changed, but that phone call become the most important one in my life. In the end, it was the catalyst, my wakeup call to living out my true purpose.

Ashley tried to reassure me; she was so calm then, and through the entire experience. She would be my solace throughout the marathon of conquering cancer. As we were packing to leave for the hospital, my good friend Justin stopped by. He's a great optimist; so optimistic he believes he'll win the lottery without even buying a ticket!

Upon sharing with him the bad news he said, "Matt, all you need is a Red Bull, it will give you wings and you'll be good as new!" As much as

I wished that was true, unfortunately, it wouldn't be that simple. After telling me that all I needed was a Red Bull, Justin spoke words of life into me by saying, "Matt, it's possible you can beat this! There are over ten million cancer survivors, and if they can do it, you can do it. You're Matt Jones, you got this!"

IT'S POSSIBLE

When it comes to making the choice to "Visualize Your Victory" you need to believe it's possible. Whatever vision or dream you have for your life, know that it's possible. Because others have overcome challenges and achieved their dreams means it's possible for you as well. Too often in life we give up, thinking that the thing we want to do is impossible.

At times, I wondered if I was going to beat cancer. My head was full of doubt and there were times I felt like giving up. One of the reasons I kept pushing forward were Justin's words replaying in my head. "Matt, it's possible, you can beat this!"

It doesn't matter the challenge or adversity you're facing, you can beat it! If someone else has done it, that's proof that you can do it. Reading this book is proof that it's possible to overcome any amount of adversity you're facing. If I can do it, you can do it!

One way to build your belief is by reading the biographies of top achievers. All of them had to overcome challenges to reach their dreams. Many have faced tremendous odds that were stacked against them. Their stories prove that it's possible for you to overcome any adversity in your life.

It's possible to achieve the victory you desire.

Before we headed out on the fifty-mile drive to St. Francis' Hospital in Topeka, I had two stops to make. The first was the mall where my dad worked as a Driver's License Examiner for the Kansas Department of Motor Vehicles. Ashley waited in the driver's seat as I went to see my dad.

"Matt, what are you doing here?"

"Dad, I need to talk to you."

We left the DMV office and stood in the courtyard of the mall as I told him the life changing words I'd received.

"Dad, I just got off the phone with my doctor . . . It's not good." With tears in my eyes I told him, "My doctor said I have cancer, I need to leave for the hospital right away."

These were words no father can imagine coming from his only son. There was silence between us as we stood hugging in the middle of the mall. After what seemed an eternity, I told him, "I'm going to tell mom now." I left in a daze, and headed across town to deliver the bad news.

My mother was an administrative assistant for the local electric company. Just as I had done with my dad, I went into her office and told her I needed to tell her something. We stepped outside to be alone. Tears flowed down her cheeks as she grabbed ahold of me and told me how much she loved me and would be praying for me.

I told her that Ashley was taking me to St. Francis and she said, "Dad and I will come to the hospital as soon as we get off work." I can't imagine how they were able to get through the rest of their workday.

It's never easy when you have to share bad news. Each time I did, first with Ashley, then Justin, my dad, and my mom . . . it felt unreal. How could this be happening to me? Last semester, my only worries were how to gain more muscle, pass my classes, and save up money for a new car. Now, my worries were life and death.

The choice to "Visualize Your Victory" requires you to believe it's possible. An example of this is a metaphor used before Super Bowl XXVII in 1993 by Jimmy Johnson, the head coach of the Dallas Cowboys. He told his players that if he laid a two-by-four across the floor and told them to walk across it, almost everyone would be able to because they would have the belief it was possible.

However, if he took the same two-by-four and placed it ten stories high between two buildings, few of them, if any, would be able to walk across because they would be more focused on trying not to fall than they would on making it across (remember the race care example?). They wouldn't believe it would be possible. Most wouldn't even have the courage to make an attempt, while others would stumble and fumble, try to hold on, and end up giving up and going back to the start.

The task of walking across the board was the same. However, the player's belief of the task would change by having the board placed ten stories high.

Part of the choice in "Visualizing Your Victory" is seeing the blessing in the midst of the adversity. Believing that even in your darkest of times you're still blessed. Once again this occurs based upon where you place your focus. Even though I had been diagnosed with cancer, I still woke up that morning. I was still able to take a breath in and out. This would be an important lesson that I would come to learn and one, if you live by, will guarantee greater victory in your life.

There is always someone worse off than you are. Many times, we miss what life has for us because we get caught up in our problems. Many people think that if only their dream would come true, then they could be happy. This isn't true. Happiness, success, having peace of mind, all come through appreciating who you are, where you are, what you have, and who you have in your life. It comes from having hope and believing that a brighter tomorrow is possible.

I'll never forget the trip to the hospital. It was like I was watching a movie. Imagine a time that you felt like you were on autopilot and going through the motions. This is how it felt. I don't think either one of us said a word the entire time. As we were still trying to process that we were headed to the hospital for me to be admitted. Life would never be the same. Walking through the doors, I didn't know if I'd ever walk out. I didn't know what was in store for me. I didn't know if I'd ever see another sunrise or sunset. I didn't know if I'd ever see a full moon or a rainbow again. In that moment I realized how important the small things are in life. As I stepped inside the hospital doors the quote from the movie *Braveheart* came to my mind, "We all die, but we don't all live." Are you fully alive and making the most out of every day? Believing in the possibilities that exist all around you? Taking time to enjoy all the wonderful things life has to offer?

After checking in, we were greeted by Nurse Ginger. She was in her late forties and was wearing stylish black glasses. Her curly brown hair bounced down to her shoulders, and she had a heart of gold. I truly believe that nurses are angels on Earth. Upon seeing us she said, "Hi, my name is Ginger. I'm the head nurse and we're going to take good care of you. I want you to know that my sister had cancer and beat it! She said it was one of the greatest blessings of her life."

Hearing those words at twenty-three years old, I couldn't comprehend them. "Getting cancer, a blessing?" I repeated in my mind. I was convinced that this was the worst possible thing that could've happened to me. Today I can echo those words, "Cancer has been one of the greatest blessings of my life."

As I reflect back on my experiences with cancer, the best way to describe it is like a caterpillar going into a cocoon and emerging a beautiful butterfly. It was a transformational journey that I'm so thankful for. In life it's not what happens to you, but how you perceive it that matters. Even though I didn't realize it at the time, that day I learned an important life lesson. Cancer would be my test. I conquered it, and my story became the testimony I share.

BELIEVE IN YOUR GREATNESS

Many times it's through the challenges and adversity you experience that your greatest life's work and purpose become clear. You realize you're strong, that what you went through made you stronger, and that you can use it to help others. This is an example of what Joseph Campbell calls the "Hero's Journey". He was an expert on mythology, and found a similar pattern of the journey a hero goes on that exists in myths, legends, and stories told in cultures around the world. George Lucas used this model as the basis for the story in the movie Star Wars.

The model is of an ordinary person who gets called on an epic adventure. Along the way he or she faces many trials and setbacks. In the end, the journey transforms them and they return as the victorious hero. Each one of us experiences the hero's journey throughout our lives; it doesn't have to be some grand adventure like Luke Skywalker in Star Wars or Frodo in the Lord of the Rings. It can be a simple and powerful lesson learned that you share with others to help make their lives easier.

Through speaking I am able to use my unique talents and gifts to make the world a better place.

One way I view my adversity with cancer is through the lens of the

"Hero's Journey". Being diagnosed with cancer was my call to adventure. The process of that adventure led to a personal transformation. The ultimate victory is being able to share my story and experiences to help inspire others like you on your journey in life.

Even though adversity can make you a better and stronger person, be careful you don't allow it to make you bitter or lose your passion for life. That reminds me of a story I've heard and can identify with quite well. It's about a young woman who was complaining to her aunt about how tough life had become; she was tired of fighting and struggling.

Every time one problem was solved, another would soon follow. One day she began to mope around and gripe about how life wasn't fair. Finally, her aunt took her into the kitchen. She filled three pots with water, put them on the stove, and turned each knob to high. Once the water began to boil, she placed potatoes in one pot, eggs in the second pot, and ground coffee beans in the third pot. She then let them sit and boil, all without saying a word.

The young woman impatient huffed and sighed, wondering what her aunt was doing. Didn't her aunt just hear what she had said, why wasn't she saying anything? Didn't she know this was a pity party and she wanted the aunt to at least respond to the complaints?

After twenty minutes the aunt turned off the burners. She took the potatoes out of the pot and placed them into a bowl. She pulled the eggs out and placed them into a second bowl. She then ladled the coffee out and placed it in a cup. Turning to the young woman, she asked, "What do you see?"

"Potatoes, eggs, and coffee," the young woman said, still a bit grumpy. After all, she was in a bad mood, not hungry or thirsty.

"Look closer," the aunt said, "and touch the potatoes."

The young woman did. They were soft. The aunt then asked the young woman to take an egg and break it. The young woman wasn't quite sure where the aunt was going with this, but she obeyed. After pulling off the shell, she observed the hard-boiled egg. Finally, the aunt asked her niece to sip the coffee. Its rich aroma and bold taste brought a smile to her face.

"Aunt, what does this mean?" the young woman asked. The aunt then explained that the potatoes, eggs, and coffee beans had each faced the same adversity - the boiling water. However, each one reacted differently. The potato went in strong, hard, and unrelenting, but in the boiling water, it became soft and weak. The egg was fragile, with the thick outer shell protecting its liquid interior until it was put into the boiling water. Then the inside of the egg became hard. However, the ground coffee beans were unique. After they were exposed to the boiling water, they transformed the water and created something new.

"Which are you?" the aunt asked. "When adversity knocks on your door, how do you respond? Are you a potato, an egg, or a coffee bean?"

The young woman understood her point. She should be like the coffee bean. "How about you?" Are you the potato that seems hard, but with the smallest amount of pain, adversity, or heat, you soften and lose your strength? Are you the egg, which starts off with a malleable heart and fluid spirit, but after a breakup, or a layoff, you become hardened and stiff? Your shell looks the same, but you're bitter and tough with a cold spirit and heart. Or, on the inside are you like the coffee bean? Do you work with the situation that's been handed to you and become improved as a result? When things are at their worst, you get better. When the hour is darkest, your light shines the brightest.

As you go through life, things will happen around you and to you, but the only thing that truly matters, the only thing that counts, is what happens within you. How do you handle adversity? Again, let me ask you this question; are you like the potato, the egg, or the coffee bean? You overcome adversity when you allow it to transform you into something greater. Your answer ultimately depends upon your perception and the choice to focus on your victories or the walls in your life.

Thankfully, because of the three choices I share with you in this book I was able to be like the coffee bean. Being checked into the hospital for me was like being placed in that pot of boiling water. The hospital is an entirely different world. Even today, I can remember the sterile smell that brought back childhood memories of visiting my great-grandmother in the nursing home. As I was going through the process of checking in, I felt I was signing away my freedom. No longer would I be able to come and go as I pleased. Fear penetrated my mind, as I wondered, "Would I ever get to leave?" I felt like a prisoner as I was issued a gown just like an inmate being checked into prison is issued an orange jumpsuit. My hospital room felt like a cell and the IV's and various machines I was hooked up to were my chains. My hospital bed acted as the bars on my cell.

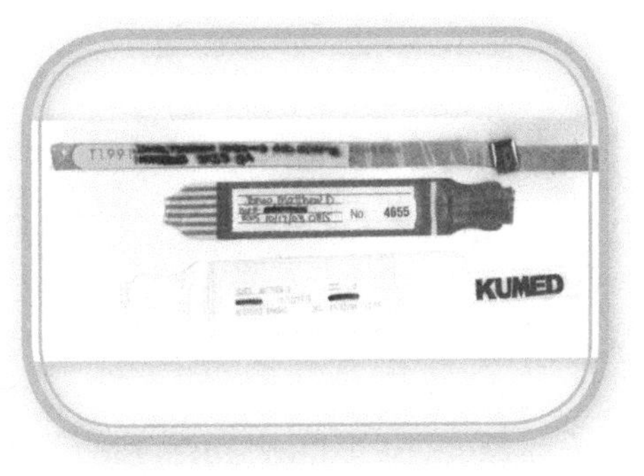

Just a few of the numerous hospital bands collected from my many stays at various hospitals.

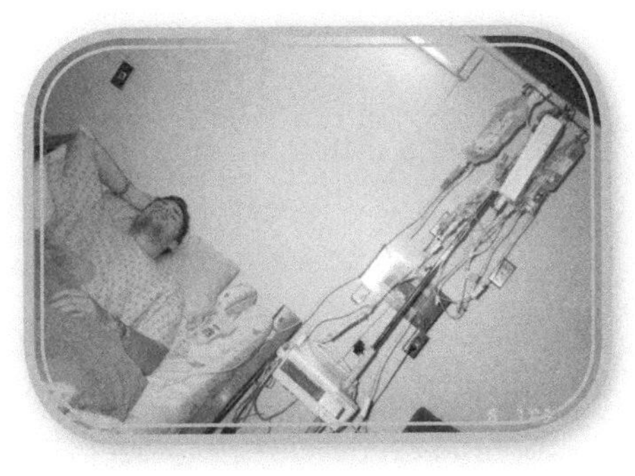

Hooked up to a machine, which pumped my various types of medicine into me.

Perhaps there have been times in your life in which you've become imprisoned by your thoughts of disbelief. Maybe you doubted that you could overcome a challenge you were facing. Perhaps you were unsure if the victories you wanted to experience were possible.

Know this, within you is the key to free yourself from the chains that hold you captive from experiencing your brightest, fullest, and greatest life possible.

Other aspects of being in the hospital are the many medical procedures you go through. One of the first I underwent was a bone marrow biopsy. It was also one that was repeated throughout my treatments. My hope is that you never have to experience one of these. It's an excruciating procedure in which a long needle is inserted into your hipbone to draw a sample of the marrow located in your bone.

The nerves in the hipbone cannot be fully deadened causing you to feel the agonizing piercing and extreme pressure of the needle entering into your hipbone. Many times I felt as if I would pass out due to the amount of pain it caused. The purpose of the procedure is to confirm the type of leukemia, how far it had progressed, and the chemotherapy needed to treat it.

I remember shivering in a wheelchair, waiting for the doctor to come into the room for the bone marrow biopsy. It was the first time I'd been alone since getting the news. The walls were gray and empty except for a single metal crucifix hanging on the wall. The floors were concrete and cold. There was an eerie and haunting silence. I waited, and waited, and waited, for what seemed like an eternity.

Just me, all alone with my thoughts and like a broken record, the voice in my head kept repeating, "I have cancer, I have cancer, I have cancer," desperately trying to come to grips with my new reality.

SQUEEZE OUT THE NEGATIVITY

Finally, the doctor came into my room to do the bone marrow biopsy. His name according to his nametag was Dr. Grinenbearit, which I assumed was of German origin. He attempted to lighten the mood by making a joke with his name.

"Hi, my name is Doctor Grin-and-Bear It. I grin while you bear it!"

At the time I didn't find it funny, but looking back I appreciate his attempt at humor. I finally lost count of how many of these painful procedures were done to me. On many occasions my mom was with me. Once, I distinctly recall lying in the hospital bed, and reaching up to grab my mom's hand, for the love and support that only a mother can give. I squeezed her hand extremely hard as the needle pierced into my bone and the pain exploded throughout my body.

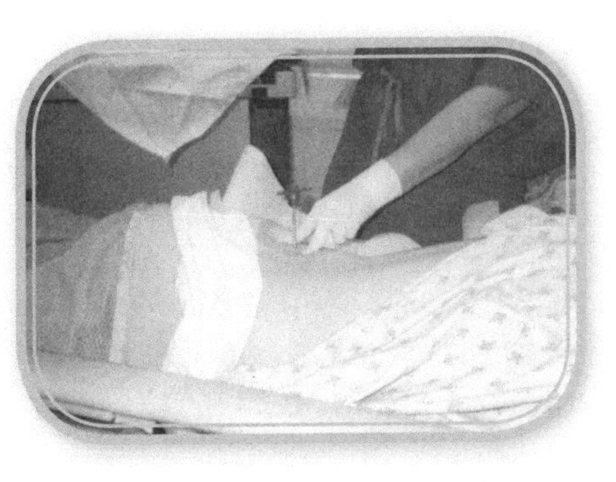

Receiving a painful bone marrow biopsy.

She recalled to me later that it felt as if I was going to squeeze her hand off. She said, "In my mind I was telling myself that you were squeezing the cancer out of your body." I said to myself, "Squeeze, Matt, squeeze." When you choose to "Visualize Your Victory" you must also squeeze the negativity out of your life.

Slides taken from my bone marrow biopsy.

Do you have any people, places, or things causing you not to achieve your greatest victories possible? Sometimes you have to make the tough decision to let go of the sources of negativity in your life. At times this includes people, places, and even things that you love but you know don't serve your highest good. The negativity caused can make you lose belief in the victory you're visualizing.

No matter how hard it was I always tried to keep a smile on my face.

After the bone marrow biopsy, the next procedure was the placement of a port into my chest, called a Groshong. It's used to administer medicine, draw blood, and dispense the chemotherapy into the body. It was an out-of-this-world experience as I lay in the operating room listening to the surgeon cut open my chest, placing the port inside of me. Luckily, the nurses gave me just enough anesthesia to feel no pain.

Pamphlets given to me describing the chemotherapy I would be given.

After surgery, they brought me back into the room where my family was waiting. The nurse asked if I would like anything to eat before they started chemotherapy. . I ordered a BLT sandwich, not realizing later that night it would come back up. This was my first experience with one of the multiple side effects of chemotherapy. I lost track of the numerous times I threw up during my first treatment. For many years I couldn't stand the sight of a BLT. However, I found that grape Gatorade comes back up green; that was a cool discovery! I started experimenting with other flavors of Gatorade, but grape was my favorite.

My first round of treatment involved two types of chemotherapy. The first, called Cytosar, was given to me for seven consecutive days, twenty-four hours a day. The second, called Idarubicin, was so powerful it could only be given for thirty minutes every other day, for a total of just three sessions or it would become lethal.

Imagine starting out your Wednesday morning as an ordinary college student looking forward to a bright future, and by night you're wondering if you even have a future. One moment everything's perfect, and in the blink of an eye your entire world can be turned upside down. You go into a state of survival. You wonder, "Am I going to die from this?" I made the decision to believe I was going to live from this.

THE BIRTH OF A NEW DREAM

When your dream comes to an end, you don't stop dreaming; instead you must dream a new dream. Lying in bed that night, I repeated, "I have cancer" over, and over, and over again. That's when I realized I had a choice to make. The fact that I had been diagnosed with leukemia couldn't be changed. Thinking back on the words of life spoken to me by Dr. McNamara, my friend Justin, and Nurse Ginger, out of the recesses of my mind came a powerful quote I'd read several years before. In *Think and Grow Rich*, Napoleon Hill writes, "Every adversity, every heartache, and every failure, carries with it the seed of an equivalent or greater benefit."

I envisioned a day when I would be able to share with people like you the message that no matter how great the odds are stacked against you, you can overcome your adversities and live your dreams. I had the vision that out of my experience someday, somehow, somewhere, for someone, some good would come from it. It gave me the fuel to keep going, the hope to face each new day. That became my seed of an equivalent or greater benefit.

If it weren't for the cancer, I wouldn't be doing what I do today. Most people upon hearing me speak assume that I'm an extrovert. Actually the opposite is true; by nature I'm an introvert. If you knew me growing up, you would never in a million years have guessed that I'd become a professional speaker who travels around the country speaking in front of audiences. As I share in my talks, I was so shy I couldn't even lead a group in silent prayer.

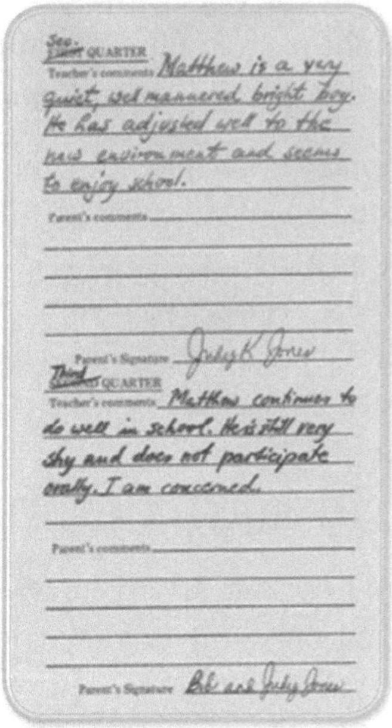

Sec. QUARTER
Teacher's comments Matthew is a very quiet, well mannered, bright boy. He has adjusted well to the new environment and seems to enjoy school.
Parent's comments
Parent's Signature Judy K Jones

Third QUARTER
Teacher's comments Matthew continues to do well in school. He is still very shy and does not participate orally. I am concerned.
Parent's comments
Parent's Signature Bob and Judy Jones

From my report card you would never guess in a million years that I would become a professional speaker.

At a family gathering, one of my cousins said to me, "When I heard you did public speaking for a living, I couldn't believe it. You were so shy we thought there was something wrong with you." She wasn't the only one. The first thing my kindergarten teacher wrote about me in my report card was, "Matthew is very quiet." That was the first comment about me in my academic career, and it went downhill from there.

Thinking back to my kindergarten experience, I'm not sure how I made it to first grade. The last thing my teacher wrote on my report card was, "I am concerned." What did that even mean? In addition to being extremely shy I also had to go to speech therapy. Even now, even though I work on it, I don't always have the best pronunciation, diction, or enunciation. Also being from Kansas, every once in awhile a "Kansas twang" comes out. That is great news for you! If I can overcome all those circumstances and live my dream as a professional speaker, it's proof that you can overcome your challenges and live your dream.

After a talk to a group of meeting planners, a young lady came up to me and said, "Matt, I want to thank you for sharing about going to speech therapy and your speech challenges. I also went to speech therapy and I've always been scared to speak in public. Hearing you has given me the courage to know that I can do public speaking. If you can be brave enough to do it, I can too."

Good Evening

* * *

Given the hard lessons he's learned, Matt Jones will be a great motivational speaker.

***Honored to be mentioned on the front page of my hometown newspaper the* Emporia Gazette.**

Those comments made a lasting impact on my life. Many times it's our vulnerabilities and weaknesses that inspire people the most. If I can overcome my speech challenges and a kindergarten teacher who was "concerned" about me, imagine what's possible in your life!

Upon hearing the life-altering words, "You have cancer," I had to have hope, belief, and look forward to the day that this tragic situation would be turned into a positive one. Like a movie in my mind, I switched the reel from "I have cancer," to a vision of inspiring and helping others by sharing my story. It's through belief that you can continue in the fulfillment of your dream, even when the odds seemed stacked against you. I had the vision of the day I would be cancer-free, healthy, and living a victorious life. The choice to "Visualize Your Victory" is a necessity in turning tragedy into triumph.

TODAY IS YOUR DAY

A great example of belief comes from the story of Mel Fisher. He was a treasure hunter who discovered one of the largest amounts of sunken treasure off the coast of Key West, estimated at over four hundred million dollars. Even more amazing was the persistence and optimism displayed by Fisher in the face of overwhelming adversity to achieve his dream.

For sixteen years he searched for the sunken Spanish Galleon ship Nuestra Señora de Atocha, which sank off the coast of Key West in 1622. During his search he faced bankruptcy and even the death of his son and daughter-in-law. Every day for sixteen years Mel Fisher would say the words, "Today's the Day!" Finally, on July 20, 1985, it was the day and they found the mother lode.

Every day you wake up is your day! It's another opportunity for you to achieve greater victory. Each day will contain opportunities for learning and growth. When it comes to belief and the choice to "Visualize Your Victory", a big part of it is your self-perception. How do you view yourself?

You may have already heard the story of the chicken and the eagle, but it's worth repeating again. It's about a scientist who comes upon a farmer's house and notices a beautiful eagle among the chickens. He's stunned by his discovery and asks the farmer, "Why is an eagle living among chickens?"

"Well," answered the farmer, "I found him when he was young and raised him with them. He thinks he's a chicken; he doesn't know any better."

This stately bird was pecking the grain and drinking from the rusted watering can, keeping its eyes on the ground, never realizing it was meant for the sky.

The scientist asked, "But, doesn't he try to spread his wings and fly?"

The farmer shrugged and shook his head no. He studied the eagle. "And I doubt he ever will; he doesn't know what it means to fly."

Like the eagle, you were born to fly. You were born to soar to great heights! However, at times we're like a chicken because we're too busy keeping our eyes on the ground, blending in with others who don't fly. You don't belong in the land of mediocrity. You were meant for greatness; you're of a higher order and being. You were meant to spread your wings to fly and soar with the eagles, not cluck with the chickens!

There is no greater tragedy known to humanity than wasted potential. You have a greater purpose, place, and position in store for your life but only if you believe it's possible. Don't allow past defeats or victories to keep you from conquering today. Don't allow the things of yesterday, today, or tomorrow to keep you from manifesting your full potential. Find your true self inside and unlock that person, so you can live the life you were meant to live. Cavett Robert, the founder of the National Speakers Association said, "Too many people die with their music still within them, never having released their imprisoned splendor." I know by the fact that you're reading this book, that this is not true of you.

There is a passage in the original *Wizard of Oz* written by Frank Baum, which didn't make it into the movie. It was the wizard telling Dorothy, "First you must put on the spectacles." "Why?" she asked. "Because if you don't wear spectacles, the brightness and glory of the Emerald City would blind you," replied the wizard.

Later on in the book the Wizard reveals to Dorothy and her friends that without the glasses the city is like any other place. It was only by wearing them that the beauty of the Emerald City could be seen. Albert Einstein said, "There are only two ways to live your life. One is as though nothing is a miracle. The other is as though everything is a miracle."

Battling cancer became my spectacles. It served as a turning point in my life as I looked at the world with new eyes. Before cancer, I had wandered off my personal path in life. Through cancer, I've been able to find my way back. I came out of that experience finding my true self. I was awakened and realized that I'd been an eagle living among chickens. If you're an eagle living among chickens, you may find it hard to recognize. Why? Because you, like that eagle, have no idea who you really are.

By getting in touch with your true self, life becomes a miracle. Each new day holds great expectations; you're excited. You see the world through eyes filled with wonder. If we aren't careful, our eyesight becomes dulled by life's mundane happenings. When you put on the metaphorical spectacles of belief you see the world as something full of new and interesting possibilities. Everywhere you look beauty, inspiration, and possibilities will reveal themselves. No longer are you confined to a chicken coop; now you soar freely through the heavens. Your view is now from above and not from below.

By believing it's possible, you transcend your challenges into victories by making the choice to "Visualize Your Victory."

CHAPTER 3:
Become a "Solutionist"

Falling asleep that night, I knew in my heart, I was going to conquer cancer. However, it would be a marathon getting there. In the end, I would come to know that the adversity experienced was a blessing in disguise.

After my initial chemotherapy, the cancer was brought into remission. I would receive two additional sessions to ensure the leukemia would remain there. This is known as the containment phase of treatment. I didn't want to go back to the hospital for my second treatment, but Ashley said, "Matt, you have to go!"

Chemo was scheduled to begin as soon as I got checked into my hospital room. However, due to my low platelet count, the Groshong port had become infected and could no longer be accessed to administer the chemo. A surgeon was called to take a look at it. Before I knew it she had taken some tweezers out of her pocket and was digging into the infected area in my chest. Pain shot throughout my entire body.

It was one of the most painful experiences in my life as a surgeon dug into my chest to remove it. It made getting a bone marrow biopsy seem like getting a paper cut. Trying to be brave, I didn't complain about the excruciating pain as the sweat rolled down my face and I grimaced in agony.

Thankfully, a nurse recognized the distress I was enduring and requested some morphine to help ease the pain. I was left with a quarter-sized hole where the port had been. It would scar over and, to this day, serves as a reminder of the many things I've endured.

The total treatment I received included three rounds of chemo, during three separate hospital stays, stretched over three months. There were brutal cycles of pain and nausea. I lost my hair. I was poked, prodded, and stuck with IVs and needles. The first hospital bill was $72,086.89, and that only cover my initial stay of three weeks!

Fortunately, I was covered under my mom's insurance. In the end, all of my bills added together would total over one million dollars!

A typical day in the hospital would start with a six AM wakeup call from lab personnel drawing my blood. Then, I would try to get back sleep but was constantly woken by nurses and doctors coming and going who were administrating tests and monitoring my progress. If I just wanted to go on a walk down the hall, it required being hooked to several machines with my bags of IVs containing medicine and chemotherapy; a trip outdoors would also include a mask and wheelchair.

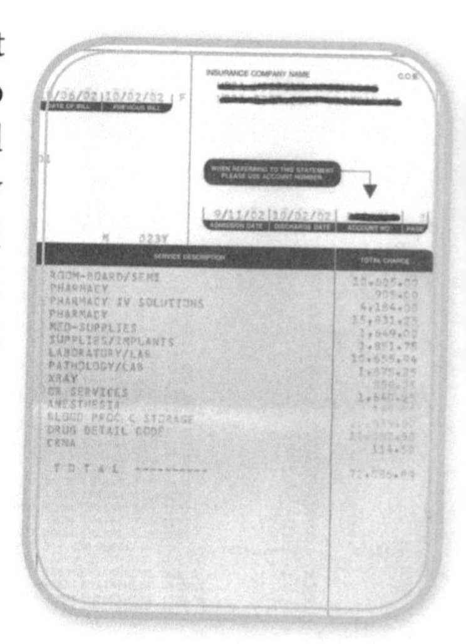

INSURANCE COMPANY NAME

WHEN REFERRING TO THIS STATEMENT PLEASE USE ACCOUNT NUMBER

DATE OF BILL	PREVIOUS BILL
[illegible]/26/02	10/02/02

ADMISSION DATE	DISCHARGE DATE	ACCOUNT NO.	PAGE
9/11/02	10/02/02	[illegible]	1

SERVICE DESCRIPTION	TOTAL CHARGE
ROOM-BOARD/SEMI	[illegible]
PHARMACY	[illegible]
PHARMACY IV SOLUTIONS	4,184.00
PHARMACY	[illegible]
MED-SUPPLIES	1,649.00
SUPPLIES/IMPLANTS	[illegible]
LABORATORY/LAB	[illegible]
PATHOLOGY/LAB	[illegible]
XRAY	[illegible]
OR SERVICES	[illegible]
ANESTHESIA	[illegible]
BLOOD PROC & STORAGE	[illegible]
DRUG DETAIL CODE	[illegible]
CRNA	[illegible]
TOTAL	[illegible]

The bill from my first stay in the hospital. Yikes!

A visit from a friend became the whole highlight of my day. Days in the hospital seemed to drag on forever as I thought about all my friends enjoying the carefree existence of college, while I was stuck in my hospital room. I missed being myself, seeing my friends, being normal. I missed lifting weights, feeling vibrant, and being energetic. I missed being able to go outside when ever I wanted without dragging around bags of medicine, wearing a mask, or being pushed in a wheelchair. Sometimes you don't realize what you have and how blessed you are until you lose it.

THE VICTORY OF REMISSION

By December of that life-changing year, I was in remission and my doctors gave me an eighty percent chance that the cancer would never come back. I felt like Rocky Balboa; I'd knocked cancer out! I was victorious! I was the champion and on the top of the world. In celebration I would drive around Emporia with the windows rolled down and blasting the *Rocky* theme song, *Eye of the Tiger*, on the car stereo. I had won! It felt as though there was nothing I couldn't overcome or accomplish.

I took profound meaning from my experience and looked for ways to use it to encourage others. I knew getting a devastating illness at such a young age happened for a reason. Treatment hadn't been easy, but I endured. I conquered cancer and now would inspire others to overcome the challenges they faced. I was now an authority on overcoming adversity. I faced a formidable foe, and I won; I had achieved victory!

Without the love and support of family and friends, I wouldn't have been able to make it through the wall of cancer. The love that poured into my soul was as essential as the medication pumped into my body. Love was like a lifeguard rescuing a drowning swimmer. The calls, cards, and visits meant more to me than anyone can ever imagine. During my stay in the hospital, I hung up all my cards; they encircled my room. Whenever the pain seemed too tough to bear, or I was feeling down, I would look at them. Focusing on the thoughts and prayers of family and friends helped me make it through the day. I received the endurance needed to make it to the finish line from those cards of love.

Many times after my talk someone will share with me about a family member or friend who is going through a challenging time and ask what they can do to help them. My advice is to continue to show them love and support by visiting them, sending them a card, and most importantly remain positive and upbeat around them.

The love that I was shown by so many people literally saved my life. You cannot survive without love. If learning the true meaning of love had been the only lesson I received from my cancer experience, it alone would be worth all the pain I endured. One of the greatest lessons I learned in my blessing of having cancer is that to love and be loved is the most important thing in life. Love is priceless; it's what makes life worth living. Without love, the world is colorless. It gives life its passion, zest, and meaning.

I am so blessed to have such a loving family.

THE CANCER STRIKES BACK

That spring I re-enrolled in college. I began to lift weights again, and life was getting back to normal. Since I had to take the previous semester off, I enrolled in summer school. I needed eighteen more credit hours in the fall in order to be able to graduate in December. I was finally back on track to fulfill my dreams. In July 2003, during the last week of summer school, my worst fear was realized.

EMPORIANS & THEIR NEIGHBORS

Turning the Tables on Leukemia

Emporia State student empowered by his struggle with frightening disease

***Article about me in the* Emporia Gazette.**

It began with what I thought was just a cold, and then it became flu-like symptoms. The week before I had received a checkup, which involved yet another painful bone marrow biopsy. The results were clear, no signs of the cancer. Then I noticed tiny pin-like red spots on the tops of my feet, ankles, and on my hipbones. This is a sign of petechiae, a red flag for leukemia; it occurs when there is a drop in red blood cells.

I didn't want to believe what I was seeing, how could this be happening again? I desperately tried rubbing the spots away with soap and a washcloth. I hoped it was just my imagination, thinking to myself, "This can't be happening, there aren't really there, I just need to rub harder." I'd already been through cancer; I was given an eighty percent chance it would never come back. What did I do to deserve this? After believing I had successfully and finally beaten cancer, knowing it had returned sent me into a downward spiral. My spirits, burdened with negativity, reached their lowest point. How many times would I go through this?

Once again the trip to St. Francis was made. Sitting in front of the desk of Dr. Hughes, my oncologist, he said, "This was not supposed to happen, I'm so sorry. Matt, this is an aggressive form, you're going to need a bone marrow transplant."

It was imperative. If I didn't get it, Dr. Hughes assured me of one thing: I would die!

It seemed like I had gone through so much and just when the worst was behind me it all came crashing down. I had fought so hard and it wasn't enough.

Life is like that sometimes. You scratch, you scrape, and you claw your way out of a situation and manage to win. You think you've reached a turning point and the future looks bright again. Then, you realize it's just an illusion. The difficult times aren't over, yet.

GETTING BACK UP

What do you do when that happens? When you've gone as far as you thought you'd have to; you've given it all you've got. Then you see there's more distance to go? That's when grit has to come into play. You've got to hold on; you've got to dig your heels in and refuse to be pushed off the path.

When the cancer came back, I faced so many negative thoughts, despair was right there on my shoulders. But I had to make a choice. Would I stop fighting now? Would I let all the work I had already done be in vain? Would I give up on myself? My answer was a resounding NO! I was going to endure until the end, even though at times it wasn't easy and some days I just barely hung on. Once again my world was turned upside down.

The plan was to send me to one of the best cancer hospitals in the world for my bone marrow transplant. But the previous October I had turned twenty-four and was no longer covered under my parents' insurance. We had been trying to find my own but with cancer being a pre-existing condition, we were denied by every insurance company we tried. Since I was without any insurance, the hospital wouldn't start the process of trying to find the donor until we had a deposit of one hundred thousand dollars. No money equaled no search.

That was almost too much for me to bear. I felt beaten. I felt like throwing in the towel.

I now faced the possibility that I might not be able to get the necessary treatment. I don't know if you've ever had this feeling, but it was as if Murphy's Law had a monopoly on my life. I slipped into a deep depression, it was like being stuck in a nightmare and not being able to wake up.

The news devastated me as I thought, "I live in one of the wealthiest countries, with the top medical treatments and hospitals in world; and I'm going to die." I got caught in the negative cycle of "Why me?" and "Life's not fair." It also meant that I had to go back into the hospital and receive more chemotherapy. It was one of the most difficult times of my life. No one deserved to go through what I was going through. I felt so helpless, so scared, and as if my life was ending before it was even getting started.

> I asked myself, "Why am I being punished?"

I threw myself a pity party. The problem with pity parties is that not many people come and the ones who do don't bring any gifts. Nurses used to come into my room and comment how it was the happiest place in the hospital; now it had become one of the most negative.

I had lost hope, lost my vision of the equivalent or greater benefit, and lost myself; I lay in my hospital bed with the lights off, the blinds to the windows closed, and any time a visitor came to see me, I pretended to be asleep. Then I met Nurse Jody, who at the time I called Nurse Ratched. She was a major pain in my rear, but exactly what I needed! Finally, she had enough, and came storming into my room. She went over to the window and pulled open the blinds, giving new meaning to the song, *Blinded by the Light*.

Nurse Jody came to my bedside and said, "Matt you need to get up, put a smile on your face, and for all of our sakes, get in there and take a shower, you stink!"

Not only did I stink physically, but I also stunk mentally. Thanks to Nurse Jody's kick in the rear I was able to visualize my victory of someday, somehow, somewhere, for someone, some good would come from my experience; I would find the seed of equivalent or greater benefit.

When making the choice to "Visualize Your Victory" it's important to move beyond just being positive or optimistic and become a "solutionist." Someone who is solution oriented and not problem focused. Ashley is a great example of a "solutionist."

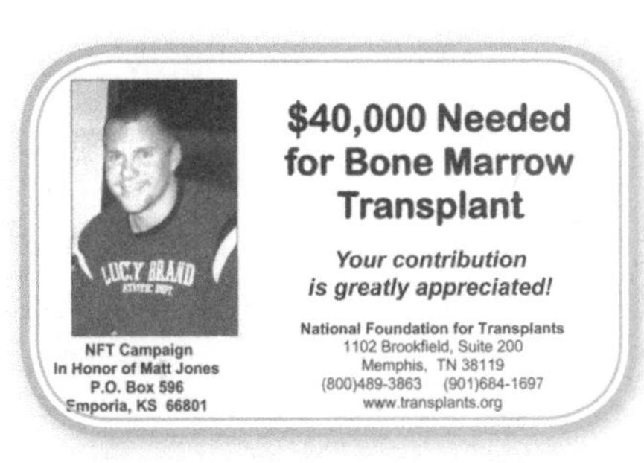

Ashley ended up raising over $44,000.

One of the great qualities about Ashley is that she's proactive and a go-getter. She discovered that I qualified for social security and Medicaid for the state of Kansas. Fortunately, there was a hospital in the state that performed bone marrow transplants, which is Kansas University Medical Center.

She researched foundations and found one that helps raise money for transplant patients. Through that foundation, Ashley led a team that raised over forty-four thousand dollars to cover the cost of the bone marrow transplant not covered by Medicaid.

Many of the local businesses hosted fundraisers.

Benefit concert for me at Emporia State University.

She was my caregiver, a full-time student, and worked a part-time job. It still amazes me all of the many things she did for me. Ashley took charge and pushed to make sure my paperwork moved through the Medicaid system – making daily phone calls, answering questions, and solving problems. Her diligence helped my approval come much quicker than it would have otherwise. She hustled and took action. As my good friend, coach, and founder of BigMoneySpeaker.com, James Malinchak would say, "She got off her assets." Even though we're no longer together; I will always be grateful for what she did for me.

Making the choice to "Visualize Your Victory" is about bridging the gap between the present reality and the desired one. It's the ability to see the larger picture and provide a vision of a better tomorrow. This allows you to become a "solutionist" and do what needs to be done today in order for your vision to come to fruition. Like a marathon, at times, achieving your victory can be an endurance event.

One of the things I do to keep myself motivated when training for my marathons is to have a picture of the city where the race will take place. I put this onto a vision board. Throughout the training process and the marathon itself, problems, or what I like to call "learning opportunities" present themselves. There are many days when I didn't feel like going out and running. I had multiple excuses why it didn't make sense to; it was too cold or hot, I was tired, or I thought to myself, "Would missing one day really matter?" One way to maintain my motivation during training is hanging a picture of my final destination and looking at it every day.

I recommend that you create a vision board. I like to make one each New Year to bring my intention and victory into focus onto the physical plane. A vision board is a collection of pictures and sayings that represent what you want in your life. I find pictures and words that I want to experience, feel, and have in my life. I cut them out of magazines as well as print images and words from my computer. Then, I glue them on a poster board and hang it where I can view it on a daily basis.

Becoming a "solutionist" requires you to focus on where you want to go in life.

BECOME A LIFELONG LEARNER

A strategy for becoming a "solutionist" as I mentioned earlier when discussing F.L.O.S.S. is to be open to learning. You must become a lifelong learner. School is never out for the "solutionist." My first class for my Master's Degree was, *The Knowledge Society*. One point that was emphasized was the need to be a lifelong learner. In John Maxwell's book *Self Improvement 101* he states, "...a single weekday edition of the New York Times contains more information than most people in seventeenth-century England were likely to encounter in their lifetimes." WOW!

Think about the amount of information you're bombarded with on a daily basis. I'm sure you've heard the expression, "We live in the information age." That's not true. We live in the "information overload age!" The result of this can lead to paralysis by analysis. This is why it's essential to keep learning to develop clarity and discernment.

Two great motivators in my life have been reading, and my relationships with other people. As I mentioned earlier, Charlie "Tremendous" Jones, said, "You're the same person today you'll be in five years except for two things: the people you meet and the books you read." Who have you met lately? What are the people you hang out with like? What books have you read recently? The answer to these questions will determine how much learning and growth will occur in your life. Are the people and the books you read solution orientated or problem focused?

Who have you met lately? What books have you read?

To stay motivated as a "solutionist" you need to keep learning. The knowledge of yesterday will not sustain you for the challenges of tomorrow. This learning can be formal or informal, but the key is to become a lifelong learner.

When I was repeating the words over and over again that I had cancer; my focus was on the wall, not where I wanted to go. The breakthrough for me was focusing on the seed of a greater benefit. This allowed me to become a "solutionist."

One way to become a "solutionist" is to dream big and ask yourself, "What's possible?" Do you remember dreaming big dreams as a kid? It seemed as if anything was possible. Hopefully, this is still true of you, and I believe the fact you're reading this proves it is. One of the greatest tragedies is when people stop dreaming big dreams and exchange them for smaller ones. This is allowing compromise to set in.

In their book, *Built to Last*, Jim Collins and Jerry Porras use the term "Big, Hairy, Audacious Goal," or "BHAGs." They describe these as goals that are "tangible, energizing, and highly focused."

In researching motivation, psychologists have found that larger goals produce more motivation than smaller ones. The reason is that they get you more excited. A large goal is more energizing and makes the necessary effort and sacrifice well worth it. The goal becomes emotionally compelling.

What's your "Big, Hairy, Audacious Goal?"

When I started training for my first marathon, people would tell me, "Matt, be realistic. Why not start out with a 5k, or at the most a half-marathon?" I couldn't get excited about running one of those; it was a marathon that got me juiced. I was willing to do whatever it took to

Crossing the finish line of the Rome Marathon.

reach my goal of completing a marathon because it was my "Big, Hairy, Audacious Goal."

Life isn't a dress rehearsal; it's the real thing. We get one shot on Earth. Stretch yourself, set a "Big, Hairy, Audacious Goal," for yourself and see what you can accomplish. Why not dream big? Life is too short and too precious to live small. Instead, live life all out, holding nothing back; fulfill those big dreams you have!

Remember, it's better to have tried and come up short than never to have tried at all. What if the Wright brothers gave up on their big dream of flight or Martin Luther King Jr. gave up on his dream of racial equality? James Allen wrote, "Dreamers are the saviors of the world." The people who change the world for good are big dreamers. Life is willing to give you whatever you settle for. So be careful what you bargain for.

THE POWER OF FAITH

One last characteristic of a "solutionist" is faith, which is the evidence of things unseen. When I made it my vision to find a seed of an equal of greater benefit from my cancer, the odds and conventional wisdom were stacked against me. The only evidence that it would be possible was my faith.

When you're dealing with adversity, faith becomes a major factor in overcoming it. Merriam-Webster dictionary defines faith as, "Something that is believed especially with strong conviction." You must have faith that you can achieve victory over your adversity. With every fiber of your body you must hold onto the conviction it's possible. Put faith into practice by believing you'll be restored and that life will become richer and fuller beyond your wildest imagination.

Practicing faith is also about putting our trust in someone or something outside of us. For many this is a higher power. Personally, my journey with cancer allowed me to grow spiritually and have greater faith in my personal belief in God. I also learned that I had to put faith in my doctors, nurses, and the treatment that was prescribed for me, trusting that everything would work out for my highest good.

Faith is really a simple concept and something we practice every single day. Do you understand how electricity fully works? Probably not, yet, every time we flip on a light switch we have faith the light will come on. How about driving and having faith that the other person will stay in their lane or not run a stoplight?

Besides having faith in conquering cancer I also had faith that something good would come out of the situation. This is the belief I had from day one and it carried me through the dark nights: having faith that all things work together for a greater good. Corrie Ten Boom said, "Faith is like radar that sees through the fog."

Making the choice to "Visualize Your Victory" happens by seeing the possibility and believing in it, like when Dr. McNamara told me, "You can get through this." Whatever adversity or challenge you are now going through or will go through, know that not only can you get through and survive, but also thrive because of it. Recognize that it's possible to overcome it, just like my friend Justin, telling me that it was possible for me to conqueror cancer.

Making that choice to "Visualize Your Victory" requires recognizing that perception is reality. Knowing it's not what happens to you that matters, but how you perceive it. Realizing that adversity can be a blessing or a curse, depending upon how you view it.

A big reason I was able to visualize my victory was getting ahold of the book *Man's Search for Meaning* by Dr. Viktor Frankl. This happened shortly after Nurse Jodi gave me my much needed attitude pep talk! Dr. Frankl was a Jewish Psychiatrist placed in a Nazi Concentration Camp.

I can't imagine the horrors and tragedies he experienced. He lost his whole family.

In that book, he wrote something so profound it forever changed my perception on life. Frankl wrote, **"Everything can be taken from a person expect one thing, the last of their freedoms, to choose one's attitude in any given set of circumstances."** Wow, that is so powerful! Reading about Frankl's experience helped me to see my adversity in a different light and focus on the solution.

As we come to the conclusion of choice one, think of a victory you would like to achieve. Maybe like me it's to run a marathon, or to overcome a certain adversity in your life. Below is space to write out one victory you would like to achieve.

Victory You're Visualizing: ________________________________

____

____

____

____

CHOICE TWO

TAKE ACTION

**"To know and not to do,
is not to know."**

CHAPTER 4:
Massive Action Principle

The key to success in life can be summed up in two words: "TAKE ACTION!" The second choice you must make to transcend adversity into victory and develop your "Marathon Mentality" is "Take Action." One of the things I share in my keynote presentations is that successful people are willing to do the things today that others won't do, in order to have the things tomorrow that others won't have. You may have heard that knowledge is power but it's actually applied knowledge that is power. A check given to you represents potential money. If you choose not to cash it, the check remains nothing more than a piece of paper. When you don't "Take Action" in life, you're like that check: the potential inside of you is wasted.

ONE SMALL STEP

Taking action starts with the first step. A series of small steps allowed me to conquer cancer, complete a marathon, and even write this book. Every day I went a little further, taking one more step than the day before.

You overcome the challenges and achieve greater victory in your life one day at a time. Sometimes it's one hour, or even one minute at a time. Often my goal was just to make it through the day, having the hope of being one day closer to going home. A strategy to live one day at a time is to find joy in little things. Some of those little things in the hospital were receiving mail, having chocolate pudding for dessert, or seeing a family member or friend walk through my door. Too often, we get caught up in the worries of tomorrow and it robs us of the joys of today.

When I relapsed for the first time and was told I needed a bone marrow transplant, it would've been easy to become paralyzed by fear. I knew that if I'd focused on all the unknowns and what might lay ahead, I would've never gotten through it. My doctor gave me the choice of checking into the hospital that night or the next day.

He said that even if I checked into the hospital that night they wouldn't be able to start the chemotherapy treatment until the next day. Since it wouldn't matter one way or the other, it made it an easier choice. Knowing that I had a long journey ahead of me and unsure how it would turn out, I chose to "Take Action" by checking into the hospital the next day.

I also made the choice to not worry about my treatment that was starting the next day. That night I celebrated life by going out to eat at one of my favorite restaurants and watching a movie. Live fully this day, it's all you'll ever have. Life is to be lived in the present. Why put off until tomorrow what you can do today? Yesterday is gone and tomorrow is yet to come. Live fully in this day, for it is a miracle.

Yesterday is a cancelled check and tomorrow is a promissory note.

My second stay in the hospital was a totally different experience than my first. Many times I felt I couldn't endure another day. I'd never felt so discouraged, disappointed, and defeated. I was tested to the very limits of my life.

Celebrating my 24th birthday with my parents in the hospital.

Searching for something I could feel in control of, I stayed enrolled in college against the advice of my doctors. They tried to persuade me not to take classes, thinking it would be too much for me because of the intensity of my treatments. I understood where they were coming from, but I needed something to focus and "Take Action" on besides the cancer and my treatments.

Staying enrolled in college empowered me to withstand the grueling months of an aggressive treatment to get me back into remission in order to be able to go through the bone marrow transplant. It was my last semester and I was determined to graduate. This would require completing eighteen credit hours of college courses, which was six credit hours over the requirement to be classified as a full-time student. The most credit hours I'd ever taken up to that point had been fourteen.

My professors at ESU were so understanding and helpful as I continued taking classes while receiving chemo in the hospital.

Cancer wasn't going to have control over my life. When facing adversity, you need something you feel in control over, a victory you're pursuing by taking action. For me it was turning my hospital room into a "dorm room" as much as possible. This included rearranging the furniture, putting posters on the wall, and having a Nerf basketball goal. Doctors would even come in and shoot hoops with me.

You are transformed by the small actions you take repeatedly.

CHOOSE ACTION OVER FEAR

Many times the actions you need to take are small ones. When I speak about taking action, one of the things I share is the "Massive Action

Principle." It can be stated as follows: the smallest actions produce the biggest results. For example, at two hundred and eleven degrees Fahrenheit, water is extremely hot; by increasing it by one degree to two hundred and twelve degrees Fahrenheit, it becomes boiling, producing steam, which can power a locomotive engine.

In order to reach your goals and dreams in life, to fulfill the vision, you have to "Take Action" every single day. It doesn't matter how small it is; the key is that you do something every day that moves you closer to the vision you have for your life.

Many times in our lives, fear keeps us from doing what we want, or need, to do. When you think about it, most of the time, there's really nothing to fear. Psychologists say that we are born with two fears: heights and loud noises. The rest of them are picked up over the years. What fears are holding you back from achieving your goals and reaching your full potential?

An acronym for fear that I like is "**F**alse **E**vidence **A**ppearing **R**eal." In reality the things you fear most usually don't occur, yet you waste so much energy worrying about it in the process. This reminds me of the quote by Mark Twain, "I've had a lot of worries in my life, most of which never happened." Once again, what you focus on is what you get back.

I remember one of the first times I felt massive fear; it was Mrs. Farmer's seventh grade gym class. It was my favorite except for one thing, swimming! Not only did I not know how to swim, I was also terrified to put my head under water. Fortunately, I was put in the beginners group. This meant staying in the shallow end and even getting your own kickboard. We got to play fun games such as water basketball and polo. I actually looked forward to swimming class until the last day when Mrs. Farmer announced, "Today, class, you're going to learn how to dive."

I thought to myself, "Learn how to dive? First, I need to learn how to swim!" This meant going to the deep end, the dreaded side of the pool I didn't dare venture into. The good news: being in the beginners group, meant I didn't have to jump from the high dive; the bad news was, that I had to dive from the edge of the pool into nine feet of water!

I was barely five feet tall and had recently read about how someone drowned in his bathtub! A popular show at the time was *Saved by the Bell* and my plan was to let all my classmates go before me, thinking the bell would ring before I had to jump.

The plan backfired, everyone else had gone and all eyes were on me. Now I had a new fear, "What would my classmates think of me if I didn't jump?" As I stepped to the edge, Mrs. Farmer started the countdown, "3, 2 . . ." Why she did a countdown I don't know, because it didn't help!

I stood at the edge of the pool, shaking with fear, and in my mind I figured that I had two choices. Run home as fast as I could and transfer to a different school, or jump and drown. Ridiculous thinking, but that's how fear works. When she reached one, I jumped; on the way down I hoped that someone knew CPR, and that it would be a pretty girl! Buoyancy is an amazing thing; I popped back up and clumsily dog paddled to the edge of the pool.

As I was walking to my next class, Mrs. Farmer came running up to me saying, "Matt, Matt I'm so sorry, I forgot you don't know how to swim!" I thought to myself, "Now she remembers? I could've drowned!" She then said something I've never forgotten, "Matt, that was so courageous." As she said it I thought to myself, "Courageous? Did she not know how scared I was?"

That day in Mrs. Farmer's seventh grade gym class I learned an important lesson:

Courage is not the absence of fear, it's doing the thing you need or want to do despite being afraid.

I was able to face the fear of diving by using the "Massive Action Principle." All I did was take one step, and jump. Many times in your life the hardest part will be to have the courage to take the first step.

Bear Grylls, who starred in the Discovery show, *Man Versus Wild*, would document his extreme nature endurance events. In one episode, his goal was to get across Siberia. When asked how he was going to accomplish this daunting task, Bear responded, "Take manageable steps and keep moving." This is great advice for getting through your adversity and achieving greater victory.

Take the first step.

When you "Take Action," you keep yourself motivated, knowing that each day and each action is taking you one step closer to where you want to be. The best definition of success I have found is by Earl Nightingale, who said, "Success is the progression toward a worthwhile goal." As long as you are taking action leading you closer to your goal, you are successful.

I encourage you to visit www.Marrow.org to learn more about becoming a bone marrow donor.

The quest to find a donor was a slow, arduous road. My sister was tested; she wasn't a match. My mom and dad were tested; neither were a match. Every day, I would eagerly check the answering machine, hoping a match had been found. Each day, there was nothing but a heavy silence; it felt like my shot at life was slipping away. Why couldn't they find a match?

Finally around Thanksgiving, we were notified by Kansas University Medical Center that a potential donor had been found. I remember thinking, "Christmas came early this year." For unknown reasons, the donor didn't work out. Once again, I felt bitter disappointment and wondered if a match would ever be found. In the end, it would take eight grueling months before a donor was finally located.

PRESS FORWARD

Conquering cancer, like running a marathon, is both mentally and physically grueling. Those eight months of waiting, hoping, and believing a donor would be found were some of the longest ones of my life. The one thing I had to remember was to keep pressing toward the finish line. This is also true of staying motivated when dealing with adversity. You must always press toward the victory you're visualizing by taking action. Below are five ways to do it:

P*ursue it at all costs*

How bad do you want it? Are you willing to pay the price? Give it your all.

R*esist the urge to compromise*

Several times in my marathon with cancer a voice in the back of my head became the voice of compromise. "Matt, you can't do this; just give up." Beware of the voice of compromise.

Embrace the challenges

Along the way will be challenges. By embracing them, you can become the person you need to be in order to achieve your goal.

Strive to reach the finish line

It's not how you begin, but how you end, that ultimately matters. When you continually strive to reach the finish line, you'll find your second wind.

Seize the day

You're probably familiar with the saying, "Why put off until tomorrow what you can do today?" However, many times we live by the exact opposite saying, "Why do today what can be put off until tomorrow?" As you know, tomorrow never comes. Today is the day, and now is the time to press toward your goal.

What is one action step you can take today that will bring you closer to your goal?

Maybe it is to join a gym, invest in a book about an area in which you would like to achieve more victories, or commit to becoming a volunteer. Whatever it is, do it!

By putting the "Massive Action Principle" into practice you build perseverance. This is the building block of achievement. It's like the foundation of a house; everything else stands on top of it. In life, victory doesn't always go to the person who is the strongest or the fastest, but to the person who isn't willing to give up.

In order to turn your tragedy into triumph, you must persevere; at times when you've gone as far as you thought you needed to, and you've given what you thought was your best, realize that deep down you have more to give. A great example of this comes from a quote from the movie *The Owls of Ga'Hoole*, "When you've flown as far as you can, you're halfway there!"

Perseverance is the thing that separates the successful from the unsuccessful, because to carry something out you have to stick to it. It's easy to keep going when things are well, but the true test is when things aren't going as planned, or when it seems you're moving further from your vision. At that time, you face a decision: continue or quit. Do not quit! Quitting cannot be an option.

Many times, during a marathon and while battling cancer, I felt like quitting, but I kept going, one step at a time. When you feel like you are at the end of your rope, hang on for a little longer. If you do, eventually you will succeed.

In Napoleon Hill's book, *Think and Grow Rich*, the author tells the story of man who quit mining just three feet from striking gold. The man who bought his operation only had to go three feet before striking a vein that produced millions of dollars of ore.

Perhaps, like that man, you are just three feet from striking your own source of gold! Imagine how you would feel knowing that you gave up while being so close to your victory!

> Any amount of success that I've achieved in my life hasn't happened because I'm the smartest, strongest, or fastest but rather because I've kept plodding along.

HITTING THE WALL

One area where the "Massive Action Principle" is important is when you hit the wall. This term comes from running. I describe it as when your body becomes weak, your sprit is beaten down, and your will is drained. When you hit the wall, your legs feel like Jell-O, you grasp for air, and you wonder if you can go any further. Maybe you have never experienced this wall on a physical level, but there's also a mental wall. This is the inner barrier where you run out of willpower emotionally and think you cannot go any further.

At some point in life, we all hit the wall. Maybe you're hitting the wall right now. What do you do when it happens? When it seems that you have given everything that you have? That's when you have to dig deep within yourself and find your inner strength in order to take one more step to push through the wall. Many people who face challenges or setbacks just stop, they quit, and give up on achieving their victory.

You are not most people. The fact that you made it this far in the book is proof of that. If you keep pushing, eventually, you will break through to the other side. If you just keep going, you'll catch your second wind.

I'd like to share with you some of the words from an inspirational poem by Robert Service:

Carry on! Carry on!

Fight the good fight and true;

Believe in your mission, greet life with a cheer;

There's big work to do, and that's why you are here.

Carry on! Carry on!

Let the world be the better for you;

And at last when you die, let this be your cry!

Carry on, my soul! Carry on!

No matter what difficulty you are facing, carry on until you triumph.

By December of 2003, I was back into remission! For the second time I had conquered cancer! I did the seemingly impossible and had also completed all eighteen credit hours needed to graduate, and even got a 4.0, which was my first and only semester of doing that. I graduated from Emporia State University with a Bachelor of Arts in Communication. I realized my dream of walking across the stage to receive a diploma; what an awesome feeling! I had persevered against insurmountable odds.

It was such a great feeling walking across the stage and receiving my college diploma.

My good friend Justin said, "You beat cancer again, now what?" I replied, "Just like the Super Bowl MVP, I'm going to Disney World!" Little did I know this would be the calm before the impending storm.

I was relieved to be back in remission and to have graduated college, but in the back of my mind thoughts of the pending marathon of the bone marrow transplant to come. I was feeling great so I started thinking, "Maybe I don't need the transplant."

At Disney World, I started having migraines that became worse and worse as the days progressed. When I got back to Kansas they were so painful, it felt like an eighteen-wheeler was parked on top of my head. When I opened my eyes, searing pain flashed through my brain. I rolled back and forth in the fetal position with my hands covering my eyes and moaning in pain.

Ashley said, “Matt, something is really wrong, we’ve got to get you to the doctor, now!” My family doctor, unsure of what was happening, prescribed me pain medication and referred me to a specialist.

Later that day, I lay in bed enduring hallucinations of Mickey Mouse in my bedroom. “What’s he doing here? Wait, where am I, am I back in Disney World?” He was in the middle of the bedroom floor and kept singing *It’s A Small World* over and over, torturing me.

I remember yelling at the imaginary Mickey Mouse, “Stop! Go away! Stop! Leave me alone! Just stop!” I knew that something was wrong, very wrong.

Acute Myeloid Leukemia is one of the worst blood cancers because it can aggressively spread to the cerebral spinal fluid. When I got to the hospital and found out the specialist was a neurosurgeon, I realized how dire my situation was. They ran a brain scan and told me, “Come back Monday for the results.” It seemed like one bad thing after another. I kept asking myself, “When will this all end?” It felt as if as soon as things got a little better, something worse would happen. I remember my grandmother saying, “This too shall pass.” I began to wonder if that was true.

Before checking out to go home, I asked if I could lie down, I wasn’t feeling good. Noticing the condition I was in, one of the nurses told me to immediately go to Kansas University Medical Center. I didn’t want to go because I felt I would be there a long time.

Walking through the hospital doors, I hoped that I’d only be there for a short stay. It would be six weeks before I was able to leave, and I almost didn’t come out alive!

DR. DOOM

That weekend more tests were run, and on a cold Monday morning in January 2004, I heard a knock. Into the room, walked Dr. Doom. She was the type of person that brightens the whole room as soon as they leave. She was so negative that if she walked into a dark room, she would begin to develop! I call these types of people "Energy Vampires" because they suck the energy right out of you. She walked over to my hospital bed, pulled up a chair, and looked into my eyes. "Matt, the cancer has come back and spread to the fluid in your brain."

Because of my positive attitude, my first thought was, "Oh my goodness, now I'm going to need a brain transplant!"

Without hesitation, Dr. Doom continued, "You have a less than ten percent chance of living to the age of thirty."

Then she got up and walked out! That's what I call a bad Monday morning! I turned, looked at Ashley, and said, "Well, maybe now I can get on Oprah."

You have to watch out for the Dr. Doom's in your life. Their negativity can keep you from taking action towards the victory you're visualizing. For many people Monday's act as a Dr. Doom.

Did you know that the majority of heart attacks occur Monday morning between seven and nine a.m.? You are probably familiar with the words, "Just another Manic Monday." This is why I am on a mission to turn Manic Mondays into Magnificent Mondays. Every Monday I send out a free Victory Email containing a quote designed to fire up, pump up, and inspire you to have a Magnificent Monday. If you would like to join me in my mission and receive your free Monday Victory Email just email me at Matt@MatthewDJones.com with Monday Victory Email in the subject line and I will sign you up. Together let's turn Manic Mondays into Magnificent Mondays.

If you would like to join me in my mission and receive your free Monday Victory Email just email me at Matt@MatthewDJones.com with Monday Victory Email in the subject line and I will sign you up. Together, let's turn Manic Mondays into Magnificent Mondays.

Upon hearing the words uttered from the mouth of Dr. Doom, I felt like an inflatable punching bag that kept getting knocked down after bouncing back up. I'd go into remission and then relapse. I'd have a high point, then a low. I'd get great news, then a bombshell. But each time, I got back up.

That's what grit is about; when things don't go as you think they should, don't give up. It would've been easy to quit and at times I was close to it.

Life is about getting back up when you get knocked down and making the choice to "Take Action" one step at a time.

CHAPTER 5:
Act or React

What happens to you in life, is secondary to how you act or react to it. You have the choice to act or react to the circumstances you experience. When you act, you are in control and make a conscious decision. When you react, you allow your unfiltered emotions to control you. Acting versus reacting is about being the master of your emotions instead of your emotions being the master of you. An acronym I created for act is "**A**bsolute **C**ontrol of **T**houghts." One I created for react is "**R**esponding **E**motionally to **A**ddictive **C**ontrolling **T**houghts."

Absolute Control of Thoughts versus Responding Emotionally to Addictive Controlling Thoughts: You have the choice to act or react to your thoughts.

Ultimately, your thoughts determine your actions. You can control your life by controlling your thoughts, which determine your actions. One reason that we react versus act is because we sometimes allow what I call our "Thought Gremlins" to control our actions. This is a concept I developed from the movie *Gremlins*, a favorite from my childhood.

The movie is about this adorable furry creature named Gizmo who is a Mogwai. When exposed to water, Gizmo produces more Mogwai. When they eat after midnight they become Gremlins that cause havoc and destruction, even killing people. Your emotions are like the adorable Gizmo, but when you feed them negative thoughts they become Gremlins. These "Thought Gremlins" consist of thoughts of **G**uilt, **R**egret, **E**nvy, **M**alice, **L**oathing, **I**rritability, **N**egativity, and **S**carcity.

Sometimes I wonder, "What would have happened if I bought into the vision Dr. Doom had of my life?" I believe if I had given into my "Thought

Gremlins" I wouldn't be here today. I think about a fellow patient next door to me. He was a firefighter who was the same age as me and had the same diagnosis, but he is no longer here. One of my speaking mentors, Les Brown said, "Someone else's opinion of you does not have to become your reality."

I had to make the choice to act or react to Dr. Doom's vision for my life. Thankfully I was able to act and chose to visualize my victory based on Napoleon Hill's quote, "the seed of an equivalent or greater benefit." Because I'd taken the action to develop my personal mastery it helped me to realize that no matter how great of an adversity you face, how insurmountable the odds may seem, or how little hope there seems left, if you can see it, and believe it's possible, you can do it. You can transform your adversity into victory by choosing to "Take Action" versus reacting.

I lived several years in Austin, Texas and one of the weirder things it's known for is having the largest urban population of bats. They can number up to one and half million at their peak. Seeing the bats at the Congress Street Bridge is one of the tourist attractions of the city. Let me ask you a question. There were three bats hanging off the bridge, one *decides* to fly away, how many are left? Did you say two? Actually the answer is all three, because there's a difference between deciding and actually taking action.

Knowing and not doing, is not knowing.

"BE-DO-HAVE" ACT STRATEGY

Renowned motivational speaker Zig Ziglar introduced the "Be-Do-Have Philosophy." In order to reach your goals and get the *have* you want, you have to *do*. However, in order to perform the *do*, you have to *be*. It's the being you get from self-development that leads to the doing and the having. It's easy to get so caught up focusing on the *have* that we forget the first and most important thing is to *be*.

Personal empowerment is about maintaining and developing your mind, body, and soul. That is why it's so essential to F.L.O.S.S. your mind on a daily basis. You can become the person that haves what you want. How? Through developing yourself daily. Read books, attend seminars, and have a personal self-empowerment plan. Brian Tracy said, "If you wish to achieve worthwhile things in your personal and career life, you must become a worthwhile person in your own self-development." When it comes to your personal development you need to "Take Action."

All three of the choices you must make to develop your "Marathon Mentality" are intertwined and together create a synergy that will catapult you to greater victory.

ACTION-BASED GOAL STRATEGY

I want to share with you something I learned from one of my speaking mentors, Steve Siebold. This will completely change how you view and set goals along with how you reward yourself and others for the rest of your life. The majority of goal setting is results-based vs. action-based goals.

Let me give you an example from sales. Let's say you have goal to make a certain number of sales. If you reach that number you are rewarded and if you don't, you may be punished. The problem with this reward and motivation system is that getting a certain number of sales is not one hundred percent in your control.

Let's contrast that to an action-based goal, which could be making x number of calls. That is something you, for the most part, have one hundred percent control over. So the results-based goal of x number of sales becomes the target but the action-based goal of x number of calls becomes your goal or the victory your visualizing to "Take Action" upon.

Let me give you another example from when I was a personal trainer. A results-based goal is losing x number of pounds versus an action-based goal of working out for thirty minutes a day, three times a week. Once again, with action-based goals you have one hundred percent control of the outcomes and achieving them.

A more effective and motivating rewards system is one based on recognizing action-based versus results-based goals. You want the goals you set to be action-based and turn results-based goals into targets to be reached but not your main focus. Rewards are based on successful completion of goals versus targets. This is more empowering and motivating because you can have absolute control over your outcomes versus having them dependent on someone else or outside circumstances.

I highly recommend Steve Siebold's book, *"Mental Toughness."* In it he writes, "Reward people for doing what they say they are going to do, based on activities they can control. The priority is still set on bottom-line results, the focus is toward high-quality, consistent execution. Reward performers for keeping their word and you build a success cycle of confidence and enthusiasm."

STAYING MOTIVATED ACTION STRATEGY

A powerful activity for staying motivated to "Take Action" is something I learned from another one of my speaking mentors, Les Brown. In a speech to a group of real estate agents, Les told them to write down three reasons why they were in the industry. Then, when they hit a rough patch or times seemed difficult, they could go back to that list to remind themselves why they chose this path. Knowing the why reminds you of the reason you made the choice to do the thing you're doing.

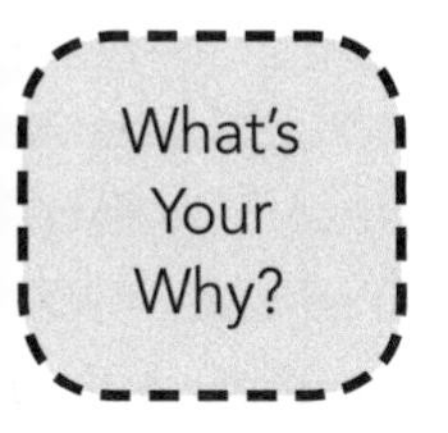

I've followed this advice in my own speaking career. I chose this profession because I feel it's my purpose, it's what I'm passionate about, and I want to leave a legacy behind. Whenever a speaking gig falls through, or it seems my career isn't advancing as quickly as it should, I refer back to this list for the motivation to continue. When I ran my first marathon my why was to prove to myself that I was healthy again. This kept me motivated throughout the training process.

Think back to the victory you choose to achieve at the end of chapter three or a victory you want to achieve. What feeling would you get from that? Why do you want that certain victory? Perhaps it's to experience more freedom, the thrill of the accomplishment, or to better yourself financially. Below is space for you to write three reasons why you want to reach the victory you chose as your goal. Reading these daily will keep you motivated to take the necessary action to achieve your victory.

Three Reasons Why You Want To Achieve Your Victory

1.____

2.____

3.____

After relapsing over and over again, in the back of my mind was fear and worry. Thoughts such as, "Is this going to come back?" permeated my mind. Anytime I got a cold, sore throat, or a spot appeared, the fear clutched my insides and made me wonder, "Is this a sign of it returning?" That took away from my peace of mind. I needed to work through it by raising my level of consciousness. Recognizing that it's a mindset, I made a decision not to react negatively. I wouldn't allow worry, fear, and anxiety to tie me up in knots and hold me captive.

I chose to "ACT" by having **A**bsolute **C**ontrol of my **T**houghts. I began to affirm that yes, I am healthy, and yes, I am strong. When those negative fearful thoughts came, I wouldn't entertain them. Instead, I replaced them with deliberate positive thoughts. I made it my business to read materials about people who had survived cancer. I spent time in their presence, developing relationships and sharing the positive energy. I found people who had passed the five-year benchmark for recovery and were into their tenth years and beyond of conquering cancer.

That was incredibly uplifting for me, and it gave me hope; if it's possible for them, it's possible for me. I didn't have time for negative people and the Dr. Dooms; it takes too much energy. Seeing the survivors celebrating life was essential.

There were times when it seemed that frustration flooded my mind with thoughts about how life just wasn't fair. But I had to move beyond that to a place where I was at peace with what was going on in my life. I had to believe that the doctors were doing what needed to be done and learned to be understanding of the fact that certain friends stopped coming around. I had to come to terms with not having insurance and looking for a solution. I had to be at peace with my new reality.

I came to accept the fact that I couldn't always operate at the same high level of energy I once had, sometimes I needed to take a nap. I had to learn to love the new me. Having peace of mind means accepting change and making room for what's new in life. The author of one of my favorite books, *As a Man Thinketh*, is James Allen; he calls this peace calmness of mind, it is the result of self-control and a sign of wisdom.

As you exert control over your mind and actions, you will develop peace in knowing you're the master of your life. Through your choices, you are designing your reality. You are the painter of the canvas of your life. No matter what happens to you, it can be overcome. You can triumph and reach your full potential.

TWO-FRONT WAR

The fact that the leukemia came back and spread to the fluid in my brain meant we were now fighting the cancer on two fronts. For the leukemia that had come back in my body I was placed on an experimental chemotherapy, since the first two treatments had failed. Due to the brain-blood barrier, the leukemia in my brain had to be treated separately from the leukemia located throughout the rest of my body.

This was accomplished by placing a special port under my scalp called an Ommaya reservoir (a soft plastic dome-shaped device about the size of a quarter). The operation is a very delicate procedure requiring that I be sedated; if it isn't placed in the right area of the brain, infection or worse is likely.

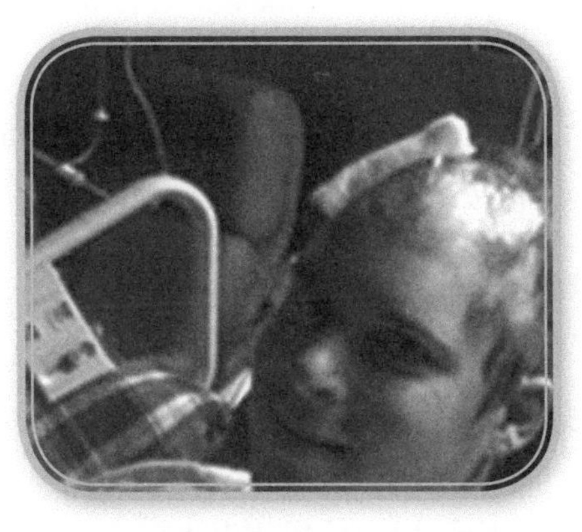

Bandage covering the spot where my Ommaya reservoir had been placed.

Before I could go through a bone marrow transplant I had to be in remission. That meant that I would have to beat cancer two more times on two different fronts. Even if the doctors were able to get me into remission, which Dr. Doom was a bit skeptical about, there was a chance my transplant wouldn't take. If it did initially take, there was a chance it would ultimately be rejected.

Talk about the odds being stacked against me! Not since conception had I faced greater odds of survival.

UNCONSCIOUS STATE

Little did I know, but the worst was yet to come. The Ommaya reservoir caused an infection in my brain, one of my kidneys began to fail, and my temperature rose to 104 degrees Fahrenheit. This lethal combination led me to slip into an unconscious state around Valentine's Day, 2004. At two o'clock in the morning Dr. Doom walked into my room. After assessing my condition she walked out to the nurses' station and told them to call my family and friends. She doubted that I would live through the night.

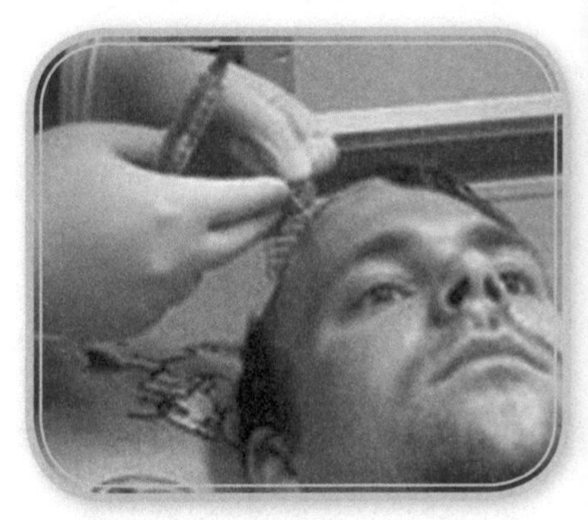

Receiving chemo into my brain via the Ommaya reservoir.

I have no recollection of that time, but was later told by family and friends about my deteriorating condition and how close I'd come to death. I was told how at first I would turn towards people when they said my name or touched me but that was the extent of my response. The nurses were trying everything they could to bring down my fever through administering fluids intravenously, cooling mats, and trying to get me to take Tylenol.

I wouldn't take the pills so they tried baby Tylenol because it's in liquid form.

However I kept my mouth clamped shut and when they were able to get some down I would spit it out. If they didn't get the fever down, Dr. Doom's deadly prophecy would become a reality. It got to the point where I wasn't even responding. Nurses would say my name and try to give me instructions but I wouldn't do anything.

At first my eyes were open but I wouldn't say anything, then I was sleeping and opening my eyes occasionally. Finally I wasn't opening my eyes at all. Doctors began making preparations to move me into the ICU.

At that time, Dr. Doom came in and pulled my parents out of the room asking them, "Do you know his wishes for things like dialysis and respiration?" I can't imagine how hard that was for my parents! What they must have been feeling is beyond explanation.

Anytime you're in a hospital with someone you love, your instinct is to tell the doctors to do whatever they can to keep your loved one alive, but my parents also knew that I didn't want to be kept alive only with machines. Thankfully, it didn't get to the point where those decisions had to be made.

Fortunately, I would get through the night. The turning point came when Ashley and Jordan were able to force some baby Tylenol down my throat. Against all odds, I started to come out of it. I came close to never leaving the hospital, so close to death that my final wishes had been discussed.

I hold onto the firm belief that cancer served a great purpose in my life. It has become a seed leading to many greater benefits, for myself and for others. One example is the fact that you are reading this book.

Even as bad as that night was when I slipped into an unconscious state, out of it came the seed of an equivalent or greater benefit. My good friends Jordan and Justin are twins. Like many families, they experienced their parents' divorce at a young age.

The relationship with their dad had become estranged and they hadn't talked to him in about four years. In a conversation about growing up, Jordan compared their father-son relationship to The Army Reserve; he got to see his dad one weekend a month and two weeks in the summer.

Later Jordan recalled to me how the night they were called to the hospital to say goodbye to me was a turning point in their relationship with their father. Seeing me persist through the night, as I fought for my life, helped him realize the importance of reconnecting with his dad.

Jordan said he distinctly remembered grabbing Justin's arm and pulling him out the door as he said, "We haven't talked to Dad in so long, we HAVE to find his office... now." It "just happened" that their dad worked at KU Medical Center. Jordan told me he couldn't put into words the feeling he got seeing the look on his dad's face when he recognized his sons standing before him.

His dad said that it was the best surprise he'd ever received. For years Jordan knew that he needed to reconnect with his dad; however, it wasn't until he made the choice to "Take Action" that he actually did.

Unfortunately, five years later to the day they reconnected, their dad would pass away from cancer. Jordan shared with me how grateful he was for those five extra years of having him as a part of their lives, because of that night. Even out of the seemingly worst situations, some good can come from them.

THE LEAPFROG ACTION STRATEGY TO SUCCESS

One thing that can help you to act versus react is to be mentored by coaches. You will notice that several of the strategies I shared in this chapter have come from some of coaches who mentored me. Coaching is what I call the "Leapfrog Action Strategy to Success." This one victory strategy has done more for my success than any other.

There are two ways to learn in life: your own experience or someone else's. Having a coach drastically cuts down on your learning curve. They've already made the mistakes and can save you the time and the pain because they know what works, and what doesn't. Why spend time trying to reinvent the wheel when a coach can show you how they made it and you just follow them?

A great example of the power of coaching is when I ran my first marathon. I signed up for Team in Training, which is the largest fundraiser for the Leukemia and Lymphoma Society (LLS.org). One of the greatest benefits of Team in Training is the coaching; they have top coaches to train you in your event. They teach everything you need to know: nutrition, what to wear, running form, workout schedule, amount of water to drink, rest, stretching, and how to run the marathon.

My Team in Training group for the San Diego Rock 'N' Rock Marathon.

Coaching doesn't have to be just a person; it comes in many different forms and venues. You can get coaching through reading books, going to seminars, and listening to audio programs.

It's necessary to get coaching because, as one of my speaking coaches, Les Brown, said, "You can't see the picture while you're in the frame." A coach can see things you can't and offer advice from their own experience on to how to improve. Many people do the same thing wrong over and over again because they don't realize they're doing it the wrong way; coaching solves this problem.

I have learned two important lessons in selecting a coach to mentor you. The first is make sure you get coaching from successful people who are getting the results that you want in your life. The second is realizing that just because your coach may be an expert in one area they might not be as strong in other areas of life or business. This is why it's a good strategy to have multiple coaches to mentor you in the different areas of your life. Someone who is an expert in physical health may not be an expert in finances or relationships.

Remember, you want to seek out coaches getting the results you want in your life. If one of the victories you want to achieve is better physical health, find a personal trainer that's at the level of fitness you desire. If it's financial, find a financial planner creating the type of lifestyle you desire. If it's relationships, find a mentor that is in the type of relationship you seek to have.

An example I share about coaching in my trainings is a metaphor about the carpool lane. One of the "character building experiences" of living in California is traffic! A blessing is when you have another person in the car with you and can use the carpool lane. If you get caught alone in the carpool lane you can get a huge traffic ticket.

Traffic, at times, can be so bad that people will go to drastic measures to be able to save time by taking the carpool lane. One trick that's used is having a mannequin in the passenger seat in an attempt to fool the police into thinking they have an actual passenger with them. I even read about someone that tried using a huge teddy bear but was caught and given a ticket!

The reason people will go to extreme measures to use the carpool lane is because it helps you get to your destination faster. This is another advantage of having a coach. No one can be successful all by himself or herself. We all need coaches who can help us along in the race of life. They also help you along when you feel like giving up by offering encouragement and challenging you to be best person you can be. A coach's hindsight becomes your foresight.

Making the choice to "Take Action" begins by realizing that you can have absolute control over your thoughts. You can choose to act versus react.

CHAPTER 6:
Law of Momentum

That night and early into the next morning, family members and friends gathered at Kansas University Medical Center praying and hoping for the best. At the time, they were unsure if I would recover or take a turn for the worse. Later, I joked about how I got ripped off in my near death experience because I didn't have any out-of-body experiences, no bright lights, no angels, not even one warm fuzzy! That part of my life was lost time; reflecting back on it now feels so nightmarish, knowing how close I came to death.

Miraculously, I recovered! One of the first things I remember was sitting on a hospital bed and wearing tennis shoes with the laces untied. I looked down, knowing I was supposed to do something with them but I couldn't remember what, or how. In my hospital room was a physical therapist and my dad. As I struggled to remember what to do, my dad walked over, and just like when I was five years old, he knelt down and tied my shoes.

I was a twenty-five year old man and my dad had to tie my shoes. As I think back, if only they would've been Velcro, that would've solved the whole problem! Today being able to tie my shoes is a victory.

After he got done tying my shoes, he and the physical therapist helped me stand up. As I stood there, I knew that I was supposed to do something but, once again, I couldn't remember what it was. They put one of my arms around the physical therapist and the other around my dad. They then took my left leg, picked it up, and put my left foot in front of my right. Then they took my right leg, picked it up, and put my right foot in front of my left; one by one, over and over, as I had to relearn how to walk.

YOU CAN DO IT

As the physical therapist and my dad picked up each leg my dad said to me, "Matt, you can do it, one step at a time son, you can do it."

> Years later, as I ran in my first marathon, those words would echo in my mind. "Matt, you can do it, one step at a time son, you can do it."

You overcome adversity and achieve victory one step at time. That day, even with the help of my dad and the physical therapist, I could only go five yards and I was exhausted. The physical therapist got a wheelchair to roll me back to my hospital room.

Two years before, my dream was to become a body builder, my world revolved around the gym and my whole identity was being the muscle man on campus. I should've been in my physical prime and I couldn't even walk five yards with the help of two other people. It was a humbling experience. Another thing I learned from Les Brown is, "You don't ask for help because you're weak but you ask for help because you want to remain strong."

One bright spot during this time occurred with my dad. He would push me around the hospital in a wheelchair, and it was a real bonding time for us. I was so appreciative to him for wheeling me around like that because it was my only way to get out of the room; I couldn't walk, and I was so weak. Those trips were the highlight of my day. We explored all over the hospital and even went to some closed-off hallways where we weren't supposed to go.

GRATITUDE

Cancer has changed Matt Jones. The deadly disease has given him a new appreciation of life.

EASON OF
HANKS

ABOUT THIS SERIES

If I can go from being confined in a wheelchair to running marathons around the world; imagine what is possible for you.

On one adventure, my dad was pushing me down a ramp, lost control, and my wheelchair was flying towards a crash landing into a wall! Luckily, he was able to grab ahold of me before I crashed! We got a good laugh out of that, and I was so grateful for that time together. It was like I was a small boy again playing catch with my father in the front yard.

The infection in my brain not only forced me to relearn how to tie my shoes and walk, but it also had other side effects. My speech was slurred, my thoughts were scrambled, and I couldn't concentrate long enough to read a paragraph.

Fear gripped ahold of me as self-defeating thoughts ran rampant in my mind. Images that my recovery would be marred, by not being able to live my dream of inspiring others through sharing my story, flooded my mind. This was one of the scariest and most frustrating times of my life. Trying to get thoughts out that wouldn't come, being confused, and fearing this would be my new normal.

The fact that you are reading this book right now is a miracle. Just think what you are capable of doing! Imagine what is possible in your life. I went from not being able to read a paragraph or write a coherent sentence to writing this book. Reading these words right now is proof of what's possible when you make the choice to "Take Action."

In the course of writing this book there were days I didn't feel like writing or I could've made the choice to do a number of other activities. It was the choice to write one word, one sentence, one paragraph, and one chapter at a time that ultimately resulted in what you're now reading.

YOU CAN GET THROUGH THIS

After being wheeled back to my room, the physical therapist helped me back into my hospital bed. Lying there, thoughts of quitting ran through my head. The negative self-talk kicked in, "Matt, just give up, you won't ever be normal again." I didn't know how much perseverance I had left within me. Then the words of Dr. McNamara came rushing back, "You can get through this." In my mind's eye I got a vision of running a marathon. It represented the ultimate endurance event; I thought that if I could do a marathon it would prove that I was healthy again.

Think for a moment about the "ridiculousness" of visualizing a victory like that. A marathon? Twenty-six point two miles? I had been a bodybuilder, not a runner. The most I'd ever run up to that point had been two miles! I couldn't even go five yards with the help of two other people. To get a crazy idea like that, I think it must've been all the medications I was on!

I needed that big victory to strive for, something that would require all of my focus and test my fortitude. You weren't meant to eke out a life of merely surviving, barely getting by, or living a second-class existence. You're meant to live a life of greatness, a life full of happiness, love, and abundance. To live a life that makes a profound difference and experiencing the magic of each new day that causes you to beam forth with passion and overflow with joy.

Life is whatever you make out of it. It can be a daring adventure, a great comedy, or a passionate romance. You are the director. It starts with the choice of the victories you visualize and then making the choice to "Take Action" on them. When I was getting ready to go through my bone marrow transplant, a nurse told me about a young man close to my age who had recovered from a successful transplant and was now back to golfing. I was so appreciative for her sharing that example and trying to encourage me. But I thought to myself, "You get to ride in a cart when you golf." I wanted to be able to do much more than just that when I got out.

My philosophy in life is to play all out; to experience as much as I possibly can in this short time we have on Earth, to live life to the utmost fullness. One of the victories I visualized while laying in my hospital bed was to travel. I've been so blessed to travel around the world to places like the Roman Coliseum, Machu Picchu, The Sydney Opera House, and a Safari in South Africa. Two of my future victories include hiking up Mt. Kilimanjaro and traveling to outer space. Where do you want to travel, what adventures do you want to set out on?

One of the greatest experiences of my life was visiting Machu Picchu.

LAW OF MOMENTUM

If you think back to science class, you may remember learning about the law of momentum. Objects at rest tend to stay at rest and objects in motion tend to stay in motion. You can visualize all the victories in the world but to make them become a reality, you have to "Take Action." This creates momentum, which ultimately leads to the fruition of the victory you are visualizing.

You Create Momentum One Step At a Time

Lying in the hospital bed, I recognized that it wouldn't be possible for me to run a marathon the next day, month, or even in a year. If I had tried, discouragement would've set in and I would've most likely given up. At the same time, I needed to make the choice to "Take Action" to put the law of momentum into practice. If all I had done was lay in my hospital bed, I would have never run seven marathons on seven continents.

Bill Gates touched on the law of momentum when he stated, "We tend to overestimate what we can do in one year and underestimate what we can do in ten years." Having unrealistic expectations can sabotage your momentum, when you don't progress as quickly as you thought you would, it can lead to discouragement and you stop taking action. The opposite is also true, when you don't take any action, because you don't think it's worth it or even possible. Both keep you from overcoming the adversity you're facing, and achieving greater victory in your life.

Realizing this, my first goal was to be able to take one step by myself; after that it was to make it down the hospital hallway and back. After being released from the hospital, my goal was to make it around the block. Two years and four months later, I would complete my first marathon.

What step do you need to take today to the get the law of momentum going in your life?

PLAN OF ACTION

One way to ensure you keep momentum going is by having a plan. In sports, there's a game plan. In teaching, there's a lesson plan. In building a house, there's a blueprint. When you go on a trip, you get directions. In life, however, the majority of people have no plan; they go along without ever taking the time to plan the kind of life they would like to live. Do you have a plan for your life? Without one it's easy to wander aimlessly, settling for whatever comes your way.

With no plan, you become like Alice in Wonderland when she asked the Cheshire cat which way to go. He responded, "Where do you want to go?" Alice said she didn't care and the Cheshire answered, "Then it doesn't matter which way you go."

In order to conquer cancer, my doctors came up with a plan. At first it was just chemo. When I relapsed, they modified the plan to include a bone marrow transplant. When it spread to the fluid of my brain, once again the plan was updated.

They had to plan out the different treatments that had the best chances of being successful. I don't want to imagine what would have happened if my doctors didn't plan for me to beat cancer. At times your plan has to be adjusted, added to, or even thrown out and a new one created. If you don't have a plan for your life, write one out. You can design your perfect life. It is a canvas and through your choices you become the architect, director, and painter of your life.

BE STEADFAST

In addition to having a plan, you must also remain steadfast. All successful people have known some level of failure, frustration, or tough times. The hallmark of success is the ability to ride out these moments and still prevail. It's having the ability to be flexible in order to persevere in the face of obstacles.

Above all it means never stopping, never giving up, and never giving in. The power of persistence is a characteristic of all men and women who have achieved greatness. It's this persistency of effort, constancy of purpose, and consistency of staying focused, which draws greatness to the individual. I remember listening to motivational speaker Willie Jolly saying, "You have to have a P.H.D. to be successful." He wasn't talking about an academic PhD, but rather persistence, hunger, and determination. As Hall of Fame Speaker Les Brown says, "You got to be hungry!"

President Calvin Coolidge said, "Nothing in the world can take the place of persistence. Talent will not. The world is full of unsuccessful men with talent. Genius will not. Unrewarded genius is almost a proverb. Education alone will not. The world is full of educated derelicts. Persistence and determination alone are omnipotent. The slogan 'press on' has solved and always will solve the problems of the human race." I persevered against cancer because giving up wasn't an option for me.

An example of not giving up in the world of mathematics can be found in the life of Andrew Wiles. He worked on a mathematical concept, which had stumped mathematicians for 350 years. No one had ever figured it out; the prevailing thought was that it was an equation that couldn't be solved. Wiles, like so many others, became fascinated by the theorem, dating back to when he found out about it as a child.

At one point in his career, he devoted seven straight years of intense work trying to figure out this tough equation, putting more than 15,000 hours into his quest. He finally broke the code. He had done it! He had done what countless before him had not. Only a small fraction of his colleagues could even understand his work, yet Wiles didn't attribute his ability to break that code to intelligence, but instead to perseverance. It wasn't because he was so smart that he figured it out. It was because he was so determined. He was so committed. He was willing to stick it out until the end.

A University of Pennsylvania study showed us something we didn't need research to tell us: the gritty are more likely to find success in the classroom, at work, and in other areas of their lives. Grit is the thing that allows you to push through the walls of negativity, setbacks, and obstacles, to find the success you deserve. Grit keeps momentum going; it allows you to continue to push through adversity.

Making the choice to "Take Action" and putting the law of momentum into practice requires stick-to-it-iveness, the breakfast of champions! In order to be successful in life or finish a marathon, you must persevere. Once again, this is when grit comes into play. It's the thing that allows you to strive in the midst of adversity and come out as the victor. It separates the successful from the unsuccessful because to carry something out you have to stick to it. When you develop stick-to-it-iveness, it allows you to finish strong. Many times in life the race is not won by the person who starts out the fastest, instead it is the one who finishes the strongest. One of the keys to running a successful marathon is pacing. A common mistake for beginning marathoners is to start out with a pace that is way too fast.

Many times this is due to the excitement and adrenaline of the race. You don't want to treat a marathon as a sprint! Doing so can cause you to burnout and it's one of the reasons why runners don't finish the marathon. If you run too fast in the beginning, you'll have problems finishing because of having exhausted your body. By pacing yourself you conserve the necessary energy to endure the entire race and ensure a strong finish.

It's easy to be excited about a project or goal in the beginning. As challenges arise and the time drags on it's also easy to lose your momentum, resulting in a lack of motivation to follow through. Many times in my life, I've failed to carry out a goal or commitment. This happens when we don't have a strong finish. It's also the case with burnout and becoming physically exhausted, many times resulting in quitting.

It's necessary to take time out to re-energize. It's easy to get caught up in the short term and make choices where you don't take into account the future consequences. One example is our health. Your present habits regarding your exercise and diet don't always immediately affect you. But a lifetime of habits will catch up with you in the end, either for good or bad. By cultivating success habits today, you ensure a successful tomorrow.

Henry David Thoreau said, "All endeavors call for the ability to tramp the last mile, shape the last plan, endure the last hours toil. The fight-to-the-finish spirit is the one… characteristic we must possess if we are to face the future as finishers."

DON'T GIVE AWAY YOUR CHIP

Here is an example I share in my talks, which I call, "Don't give away your chip." When people hear that I've run marathons around the world, they assume I like to run. Truth be told, I hate to run; I'd much rather pump iron like Arnold. However, I do like the medals you get; it's all about the bling!

When it comes to choosing a marathon, I have two criteria. First, in order to get a medal you just have to finish before the cutoff time. Second, a long cutoff time.

Running the Perth City to Surf Marathon.

For the Perth City to Surf Marathon in Australia that was six and a half hours. I assumed this meant that I had three hours and fifteen minutes to complete the first half of the marathon. To keep track of your time you are given a timing chip. It's a microchip that's typically looped through the laces of your running shoes. The chip is important because it's proof of your time and allows you to qualify for your medal.

Around mile eleven, I hear the roar of a truck and watch as it pulls in front of me. A race official jumps out and tells me, "You need to pick up your pace or you'll be disqualified." At that time he informed me about the fine details of the race; there was also a half marathon that shared the second half of the course. This meant that the runners in the half marathon couldn't start until everyone in the full marathon had completed their first half, so the cutoff for the first half was only two and a half hours! So, I picked up my pace.

My timing chip from the Tokyo Marathon.

At mile twelve he came back and said, "I'm so sorry, I hate this part of my job. You didn't make the cutoff and you have to give me your timing chip. You've been disqualified." No chip meant no medal. You can imagine the disappointed I felt when he said I was disqualified. Even in that brief moment I had a choice. At times life tests you to see if you are worthy of the victory you strive for; if you are willing to pay the price.

I didn't fly sixteen hours not to get a medal! So I told him, "If you can catch me!" They were going to have to run me over or tackle me; I wasn't giving away my chip. I started sprinting towards the start of the Perth City to Surf Half Marathon, not looking back. All I could hear was the roar of the truck following me. Finally, I got to the beginning of the half marathon where thousands of runners were waiting eagerly to start their race!

My medal from the Perth City to Surf Marathon.

Upon crossing the starting point of the half marathon, I noticed a TV crew filming the event. Since I was in first place for the first time in my life I extended my arms over my head and shouted, "Victory!" Too often, when it comes to our victory, we give away our chip. It would've been easy to accept the race official's opinion, just like I could have listened to Dr. Doom's opinion, of my reality. When faced with adversity, don't give away your chip. Later that day when they placed the medal around my neck, it was a euphoric feeling! I was so glad I didn't give away my chip!

DESIRE: THE FUEL OF ACTION

Another way to keep momentum going is by having desire, the fuel of action. A 747 jet is an impressive engineering accomplishment. It's amazing how something so big and heavy is able to lift off the ground and fly miles into and through the air. However, without fuel the 747 would never be able to get off the runway.

Achieving greater victory, like a 747, requires fuel to take off and stay aloft. The fuel for achieving greater victory is desire; it's one of the main ingredients in the recipe for success. Desire is what enables you to do the things necessary for your dream to become a reality.

It takes the desire to be healthy in order to pass on that piece of cheesecake or to exercise instead of watching TV all night long. When you have desire, the sacrifices and the amount of time required to achieve what you want are no longer issues.

You can create desire by listing the reasons why you want to achieve a certain thing. Those reasons will cause a burning desire inside of you and just like a 747, your dream will take off.

BE EMPOWERED

Your desire is maintained by empowering yourself. Let me give you an example for a marathon. Every few miles there are aid stations where volunteers hand out water, sports drinks, and nutrition bars. There are also spots where you can receive first aid for a blister or other problems. Reaching these aid stations and receiving a drink or throwing water on your head renews the spirit. Besides the aid stations, runners carried energy gels, which they would take throughout the race; they gave much needed energy to the body. This allows them to stay empowered to finish the race.

Just like a runner needs to be empowered to complete the race, in life we must also be empowered. One of my favorite shows as a kid was He-Man; it was about a prince named Adam, who was fearful and timid. When trouble was started by the evil character Skeletor, Adam would go to Castle Grayskull, hold up his sword and say, "I have the power!" Lightning would strike and he was transformed into He-Man; now he had the power to defeat Skeletor. In the same way, personal empowerment allows you to overcome the Skeletors in your life.

Personal empowerment is about developing and maintaining your mind, body, and soul. You need to have some type of personal development plan. That is why it's important to F.L.O.S.S. your mind daily. It's like Adam becoming He-Man; you're able to connect with your higher self.

MAKE NO YOUR VITAMIN

One thing that will derail your desire and momentum is becoming discouraged. This is why it's necessary to make "no" your vitamin. A major factor in motivation is how you perceive things. One of the facts of life is hearing the word "no." Your reaction to it will determine your level of success. You can allow the word "no" to destroy your resolve, or to empower you. Instead of being discouraged, make "no" your vitamin. Successful people realize that every "no" means they are one stop closer to hearing a "yes."

In his book, 25 Secrets to Sustainable Success, Phillip C. Richards wrote: "To succeed at the top level in the financial services industry, a person needs to get twenty thousand rejections in their lifetime." How many "no's" are you willing to hear before getting a "yes" when it comes to the victories you desire to achieve?

You have probably heard of Colonel Sanders who founded Kentucky Fried Chicken. He received over one thousand "no's" before someone agreed to use his fried chicken recipe. Or maybe you've heard Thomas Edison's quote about not failing but finding ten thousand ways that don't work. Each of these men understood the value of making "no" their vitamin.

Below is a list of successful people who made "no" their vitamin:

— Stephen King's first book, *Carrie*, was rejected thirty times.

— Warren Buffet was rejected from Harvard Business School.

— Donald Trump couldn't find a single bank to finance his first big investment project.

— John Grisham's first novel, *A Time to Kill*, was rejected by sixteen agents as well as a dozen publishers.

— Jack London received six hundred rejection slips before selling his first story.

— John Creasey received seven hundred and forty three rejections slips, but to date, over six hundred million copies of his books have been published.

— Margaret Mitchell's book, *Gone with the Wind*, was rejected by thirty-eight publishers.

— Winston Churchill lost every election until he was elected Prime Minister at age sixty-two.

— Elvis Presley was fired from the Grand Ole Opry after one performance.

A great quote to write down and memorize is one I learned from Jack Canfield, co-creator of *Chicken Soup for the Soul*, "Some will, some won't, so what, someone is waiting."

MOVE BEYOND THE PAST

Another way momentum is stifled is by being held down with past mistakes, beliefs, and failures. When this happens our past becomes a chain that imprisons us. Instead of enjoying the present and working to better our future, we live in the past. Some people get lost in the "good old days." They relive past glories instead of creating new ones.

When I started lifting weights again after my cancer treatments, I was frustrated that so much of my strength was gone. It was embarrassing seeing women lifting heavier weights than I was.

My breakthrough came when I made peace and chose to move beyond the strength I had pre-cancer. It was the realization and accepting the fact that I would never be at the same physical level I once was.

It would've been easy to use that as an excuse not to work out anymore. Instead I choose to embrace and accept the new me. Maybe I wouldn't become a professional bodybuilder, but that didn't mean I couldn't still workout and have my best body possible.

Many people aren't willing to move beyond their past; they're forever stuck in it. Others hold onto guilt, shame, and regret. Don't beat yourself up over the past; it's gone forever. Instead, move on with your life and learn from past mistakes or as I like to call them "learning and growth opportunities."

How do you move beyond the past? Forgive yourself and forgive others. Let go of grudges. Release by deciding not to hang on to the past anymore. Create greater success by climbing higher mountains. Work toward greater achievements and experience new things. Always strive to re-invent yourself through constant growth and personal development. The reason why it's essential for you to move beyond the past is because it becomes a prison for those who live in it.

You also move beyond the past by making the choice to "Take Action" and press forward to the victory you're visualizing. Quitting simply cannot be an option for you. There were many times during the marathon of cancer and the marathons I ran that I felt like quitting, both physically and mentally, but I kept going. I told myself, "Just one more step, Matt." When you feel like quitting, try to hang on for just a little longer. Do that, and eventually you will succeed; this is having grit, this is putting perseverance into action.

Let go of the past in order to receive what the future holds for you.

ACTION LOOP

When it comes to keeping momentum going, it's important to close the loops of action. An "Action Loop" is the process of beginning and closing an action. Whenever you start an activity a loop is opened. An open "Action Loop" is an action that has been started and has yet to come to a resolution. An example is clutter around the house. Closing an "Action Loop" is the completion of the action you started.

Think of the feeling of unease that comes from having a sink of dirty dishes versus the feeling that comes when the loop of action is closed by washing them. The mind seeks to bring things to resolution, as unclosed loops cause anxiety. During my marathon of cancer I was in remission for the second time, but still waiting for a donor. That loop was still open and it wasn't until my donor was discovered, and the bone marrow transplant was successful, that I was able to close it.

Below is space to write down three loops in your life that you would like or need to close:

1. ____

2. ____

3.____

ACTION CYCLE

To close out part two, and the second choice to "Take Action," I would like to share with you what I call the "Action Cycle." This consists of three parts that allow you to overcome adversity and achieve greater victory. One of the keys to the "Action Cycle" is to eliminate the word and idea of *failure* from your vocabulary and mindset; instead replace it with this powerful affirmation, "I can only learn and grow."

Here are the three parts of the "Action Cycle:"

1. Take Action
2. Get Feedback
3. Make Adjustments

Once you go through the cycle, you repeat it over and over again until you reach your desired victory. As I have heard several people say, "You don't have to be great to get started but you have to get started to be great."

When it comes to overcoming adversity and achieving greater victory, there is no secret or magic bullet. It comes down to the two words of choice number two: **"Take Action."** This is what separates the successful from the unsuccessful. Too often people get stuck in the bleachers watching others play the game of life. This is why I think reality TV shows are so popular. People are living their lives vicariously through someone else.

It reminds me of the story of a guy walking down the street and came across a porch with an old man in a rocking chair and his dog. The guy noticed that the dog was whimpering and asked the old man, "What's wrong with your dog?" The man said, "Oh, he's laying on a nail." The guy responded, "Why doesn't he move?" The old man replied, "Because it doesn't hurt enough."

You make the choice to "Take Action" by taking that first step, applying the "Massive Action Principle," and choosing to act versus react in order to keep your momentum going. Below is space to write down one thing for you to "Take Action" moving you closer to your victory.

Your Action Step:

____

____

____

By making the choice to "Take Action" you give wings to the victory you're visualizing.

CHOICE
THREE

ELEVATE YOUR ATTITUDE

"The feelings you feel, the thoughts you think, and the words you speak, determine the life you live."

CHAPTER 7:
Embrace the Adversity Principle

Just like I gradually and steadily progressed one step at a time in my pursuit of a marathon; I gradually and steadily progressed in my treatment, one step at time. In the same way you overcome adversity and achieve greater victory one step at a time. Six weeks after being admitted, I was back in remission, and a bone marrow donor had been found! I convinced my doctors to let me go home for a week before coming back for my bone marrow transplant. Being given the green light to leave the hospital for a week was a lifesaver!

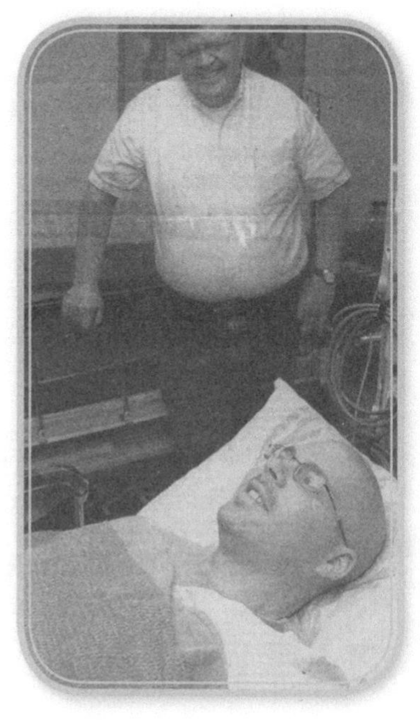

My dad watches as I'm taken to the radiation department for one last treatment before my bone marrow transplant. The only time I was able to leave the bone marrow unit was when I was receiving radiation.

That week was a series of tests, preparation, and work ups for the transplant. Because the leukemia spread to my spinal fluid, I would have to go through full body radiation. This would require three rounds of radiation for forty-five minutes a day with a day off between each treatment.

Part of receiving full body radiation required a special consultation with the radiologist. This consisted of telling me why it was necessary, what it entailed, and the numerous possible side effects. Upon leaving, I was given a pamphlet of multiple things that could occur, including bone density loss, glaucoma, and becoming sterile. When I initially got diagnosed and before my first chemo preparation I asked the doctor if I should visit the sperm bank. He said not to worry and that it wouldn't affect me that way; they needed to start the chemo right away. Even as a young man, I looked forward to having my own biological children, so I scheduled a visit to the sperm bank before I started radiation.

The only person available to take me was my mom. That, to say the least, was a little awkward. My mom is an absolute saint and I echo the words of Abraham Lincoln who said, "Everything I am and everything I hope to be I owe to my dear angel mother." She is a very godly woman; I've never heard her say a discouraging word about anyone or say a curse word.

At the clinic, I received bad news. The doctor said, "You are already sterile, there's nothing we can use here." My mom hugged me and said, "I'm so sorry, Matt." He said it was most likely due to all the previous rounds of chemotherapy that I'd gone through. Since my first treatment I'd gone through eight different rounds.

When I got that news, I had to make a choice. At first, I had resentment towards the doctor who said I didn't need to store some of my sperm before I started chemo. Several people later even suggested the possibility of suing the hospital. The reality is, that doctor saved my life. Perhaps I was already sterile before the chemo, there's no way of knowing. The one thing I do know, is that if I'd hung onto that it would've kept me from growing, leading to a prison of resentment. By making the choice to elevate my attitude, I'm able to belief believe that all things happen for the greater good.

I was scheduled to go back to the hospital on Monday. That Friday I had one final consultation with one of the bone marrow transplant doctors, who was part of the team that was treating me, we had fired Dr. Doom. The last thing he said before we left was, "One in four people going in for a bone marrow transplant won't make it out of the hospital. See you on Monday." And I thought we had fired Dr. Doom!

ELEVATE YOUR ATTITUDE

The third choice you must make when it comes to developing your "Marathon Mentality" to overcome adversity and achieve greater victory is to "Elevate Your Attitude." William James said, "The greatest discovery of our generation is that we can alter our lives by altering the attitudes of our mind."

One common denominator of successful and happy people is a positive attitude. Though it's common sense, it isn't always common practice. Some people may say it's cliché and too "Pollyanna," but it was one of the main reasons I conquered cancer and have been able to run marathons around the world. A positive attitude helps you see the solution and make the choice to "Elevate Your Attitude."

Numerous studies have shown that people who have a positive attitude are not only happier, but also heal faster. One of the keys in overcoming challenges is your attitude. Motivational speaker Keith Harrell said, "A positive attitude is the foundation of success; it's your most priceless possession, most valuable asset, and determines your overall quality of life. Your attitude today determines success tomorrow."

In order to win the race of life you must have a positive attitude. Here are ten ways to have a positive attitude to help you "Elevate Your Attitude" and achieve greater victory:

1. Positive self-talk
2. Positive affirmations
3. Positive conversations
4. Positive relationships
5. Positive physiology
6. Positive greetings
7. Positive humor
8. Positive quotes
9. Positive visualizations
10. Positive environment

POSTTRAUMATIC GROWTH

Having a positive outlook allows you to experience one of the major benefits of "Elevating Your Attitude" which is seeing the benefits in the midst of adversity. Emerging research in the area of Positive Psychology supports that the majority of people going through traumatic experiences gain positive benefits. This is known as Posttraumatic Growth or PTG. Napoleon Hill was far ahead of his time when he penned the words of the one quote that gave me my victory to visualize when I was first diagnosed. "Every adversity, every heartache, and every failure carries with it the seed of an equivalent or greater benefit."

In order for you to see the benefits you must make a choice to see them. One of my favorite quotes is by Charles Swindoll, who said, "The single most significant decision you can make on a day to day basis is your choice of attitude." The first time I went through my treatments, my choice was an optimistic and positive attitude, when I relapsed and learned I needed a bone marrow transplant it became negative. Thanks to Nurse Jody's kick in the rear I was able to elevate my attitude and learned that it's not the circumstances that matter, but rather the meaning you give those circumstances. Every day you make the choice to have a positive or negative attitude.

Something I have recently come to understand is that making the choice to "Elevate Your Attitude" is moving beyond just having a positive attitude, towards having a proactive positive attitude. If you remember from chapter three, I call this becoming a "solutionist." Once again a "solutionist" means you're solution-oriented, not problem-focused. As a "solutionist" you are focused on where you want to go, focused on your victory.

Instead of asking the question, "What's the problem?" Ask yourself, "What's the solution?"

Part of choosing to "Elevate Your Attitude" requires having a sense of humor. You may have heard of Norman Cousins, he wrote *Anatomy of an Illness*. He claimed to have healed himself from what doctors thought was an incurable illness through laughter. Laugher also reduces stress and enhances one's quality of life. These benefits have caused several cancer institutes to offer laughter therapy.

Like Norman Cousins, I recommend you practice laughter therapy. Share jokes with your family and friends; read funny stories and watch comedies together. One of the comments I get after my talks is how infectious my laugh is. People are always coming up to me saying they love my laugh and wish they could start their Monday morning meetings hearing it. Laughter is a choice. I choose to find the humor in life.

One of the most precious treasures in life is laughter.

The first time I received my experimental chemotherapy was during the start of the Big 12 Championship. Kansas University Medical Center is the teaching hospital for Kansas University. Their mascot is a Jayhawk and their school colors are crimson and blue.

I didn't realize how much school spirit the hospital had until they brought in the chemo; it was Jayhawk blue! The bag came with a biohazard sticker on it and the nurses wore protective gloves, masks, shoes, and gowns. One of the advantages of being in the hospital, at least for a man, is that they give you a hospital urinal. You don't have to wait for a commercial if you have to go; you can just go by the bedside. It's the greatest thing for a guy when it comes to the TV since the remote control.

Because the game was about to start, I wasn't paying attention when the nurse said your urine might change color. I didn't think much more of it until later in the game when I had to go. There's a saying in Kansas about bleeding Jayhawk Blue. That day I wasn't bleeding Jayhawk Blue; I was peeing Jayhawk Blue! That was an experience!

I could've allowed urinating blue to freak me out, but by elevating my attitude through a sense of humor I was able to laugh at it. A few years later I got the opportunity to speak on the same stage as Bill Self, head coach of the Kansas Jayhawks basketball team. I shared that story as well as encouraging Coach Self to win a National Championship, which they did three years later!

Upon hearing the words of my doctor saying one in four people wouldn't leave the hospital after a bone marrow transplant, my mom began to cry. I'm sure those words took her back twenty-two years earlier when she brought my younger sister Joanna, who had been diagnosed with epilepsy, to Kansas University Medical Center to run some tests. My dad was in the Navy and deployed in the Pacific Ocean.

My sister Joanna.

During the night, my sister had a seizure and passed away. I cannot imagine the hurt and pain my mom experienced, being told at the age of twenty-nine that her two-year-old daughter had passed away in the middle of the night. She was alone, her husband thousands of miles away serving his country. Now she was hearing the doctor say her only son might not leave the hospital.

Though I'm sharing my story, it's so much more than just mine. It's my mom's, my dad's, and your story. Each and every one of us experiences adversity in our lives. Sometimes the adversity is overwhelming, like I experienced, and sometimes its life's little challenges that stack up one upon another. Muhammad Ali said, "It isn't the mountains ahead to climb that wear you out; it's the pebble in your shoe." Research backs up his quote in finding that the small things cause more stress in our lives, because they happen more frequently and build one upon another.

EMBRACE ADVERSITY

By making the choice to "Elevate Your Attitude" you realize that the adversity you experience in your life can be beneficial. Biologists discovered that a lack of obstacles, challenges, and hardships are not advantageous and can lead to limited growth and development for plants and animals. They refer to it as "Adversity Principle." One way you make the choice to "Elevate Your Attitude" is to embrace this principle.

Adversity Principle: You grow stronger through challenges.

An example of the "Adversity Principle" can be seen from my days of bodybuilding. By placing stress on the muscles through lifting weights, the muscles are broken down and grow back stronger and bigger. The same is true for you; when you embrace adversity, it makes you a better and more effective person.

Remember the story of the young lady and her aunt who boiled the egg, potato, and coffee bean? That was the "Adversity Principle" in action.

When you look at the defining moments of great people, you find they came at the time of their greatest adversity. For Abraham Lincoln it was the Civil War, for Lee Iacocca it was the turnaround of Chrysler, and for Mother Teresa it was the poverty in India.

William Ward, a noted editor, author, and speaker, once said, "Adversity causes some men (women) to break, and others to break records." The difference is whether or not you embrace it. My defining moment came when I had cancer at such a young age. I could have easily been broken by it, but instead I embraced the adversity, and in doing so discovered within myself an inner strength. You too will discover that inner strength by embracing the adversity you face.

> **"Life is a grindstone, and whether it grinds you down or polishes you up is for you and only you alone to decide."**
>
> **— Cavett Robert**

One of the benefits of having cancer and facing my own mortality, at such a young age was the realization of how precious every moment of life is. We are here one moment and gone the next. So often, we take life for granted and instead of really living it to the fullest we just go through the motions.

To paraphrase Henry David Thoreau, "The majority of men and women live quiet lives of desperation." This is true of too many people. The reality is, everyone is terminal, and it's called life. None of us knows how long we have on Earth. This is why it's so important to live realizing what a precious gift each moment is.

> By making the choice to "Elevate Your Attitude" you live life to the max!

It's easy to get so caught up in all the hustle, bustle, and petty things of life that we miss out on living. What can you do today to live your life to the fullest? What would it take to close your eyes at the end of the day knowing you lived to your full potential? How can you make this earth a little better today? Maybe it's giving someone a smile or making them laugh, maybe it's the courage family and friends see from you as you overcome adversity, or maybe it's using your special talents to be of service to others. Yesterday is a canceled check, tomorrow is a promissory note; all you have is today.

BONE MARROW TRANSPLANT

When I first heard that I needed a bone marrow transplant, I had no real idea of what it entailed. Thoughts of my body being cut open and pain flashed across my mind. It was so unreal that in my early twenties I would have to get a transplant.

The first part of the process in getting a bone marrow transplant is wiping out your immune system. The reason this must be done is because that is where the leukemic cells are formed. The idea is for your donor's bone marrow cells to from a new immune system free of the leukemic cells.

The immune system is destroyed through high doses of intense chemotherapy. It was so toxic that a catheter had to be placed so that none of it would store in my bladder, which could lead to bladder cancer. Getting that thing inserted was one of the worst experiences in my life. The procedure was scheduled for the morning and I mentally psyched myself up for it. Every time someone knocked on the door, I got myself psyched up. It ended up not happening until evening! The anticipation was almost as bad as the actual procedure.

A year after my bone marrow transplant, I was invited to give a talk along with the head doctor of the bone marrow unit to the first year medical students at the hospital. One of the questions they asked was, "What was one of the worst experiences you went through?" I shared with them about having to get the catheter.

After the talk I was walking with the doctor to his office. He said to me, "Oh, by the way we no longer make patients get a catheter. We just make sure they get up every hour to use the bathroom. You were the last one to have a catheter placed." I couldn't believe he said that!

For the full body radiation, a machine called a Cobalt Theratronics 780c was used to bombard me with gamma rays, killing all of my bone marrow. I had hoped to be turned in the Incredible Hulk; instead the combination of the two made me a ghostly pale white, without hair anywhere on my body, and turned me radioactive! Instead of becoming the Incredible Hulk, I became like the lead character for the movie *Powder*.

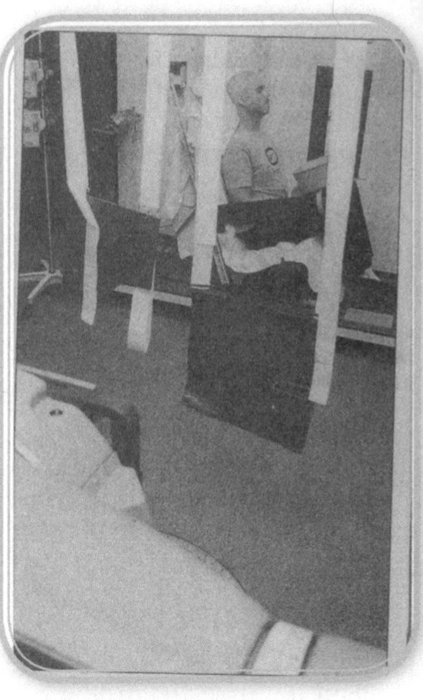

The chair I sat in while being blasted by radiation.

Once the immune system is eliminated, the body has no way to fight infections; even the common cold could be deadly. The KU Med Center bone marrow unit consisted of four rooms in an isolated wing of the hospital; visitors had to follow a strict protocol when coming to visit. Many times I would be the only person in the unit.

One of the few people who stayed in the unit with me was also from my hometown of Emporia. His name was Charles and he was in his early fifties. One of his favorite things to do in life was ride his Harley Davidson motorcycle. In the hospital he always wore a Harley bandana.

One thing I'll never forget about him was his sense of humor. He was always cracking jokes and laughing. He was a hoot! One time we attended a banquet for bone marrow transplant recipients. He commented, "All this great food but I can't eat any of it because I don't have my teeth anymore!" Unfortunately, his cancer came back and he ended up passing away.

Another thing about being in the bone marrow unit is that you couldn't have overnight visitors. That was one of the hardest times for me; it got so lonely spending the nights by myself in the hospital room and it felt like being in solitary confinement. Before, either my mom or other family members and friends would spend the night with me. The days and nights seemed to drag on. Mentally, it was straining and I constantly had to make the choice to elevate my attitude. Some days I was more successful than others.

The minimum amount of time in the hospital for a bone marrow transplant was one month. I heard stories of people having to stay more than six months, and some, who never walked out. I was determined to stay no longer than a month and told my doctors, "I am only going to be here for one month." They replied that my goal was very unlikely and I should expect to be in the hospital longer than that. Upon hearing them say that, I made the choice to elevate my attitude and visualize my victory of leaving in one month's time.

At one point there was another patient in the unit who couldn't handle it; he checked himself out. I was ready to join him. One of my nurses, who I swear was an ex-Army Drill Sergeant, sternly convinced me to stay. She told me, "He is making a bad decision; he'll be back to the hospital one way or the other." The implication was that by leaving, he was putting his life in jeopardy. She then added, "Plus, your condition is much worse than his!"

Some people rush their treatment and check themselves out, only to return much sicker; or they die because they check out against their doctor's orders. I knew exactly how that man felt, because I had often felt the same way. Sometimes you think you're going crazy, but I knew I had to be patient with the process. I learned from him; I wanted to leave when it was truly right, not when impatience told me to.

While watching him leave I was reminded of my previous six-week stay in the hospital. There had been a girl on the same floor as me who was getting to go home. As I watched her leave the only thing I wanted at that time was to be able to leave as well. It was physically and emotionally painful, seeing her bid goodbye to the walls that enclosed me. I longed to climb into the car that was taking her home and have it take me home as well.

That's when I realized I had a choice. Even though I couldn't change my circumstances, I could elevate my attitude. I then make the choice to "Take Action" and went to the window in my hospital room and looked up and seeing a car that was leaving, visualized my victory of one day ben able to leave.

By embracing the adversity principle you make the choice to "Elevate Your Attitude."

CHAPTER 8:
The Magic is in the Moment

One of the people who made a big difference in my time at KU Medical Center was Nurse Margo. Every time she walked into my hospital room she had a smile on her face; she was the type of person that brightens the whole room as soon as she entered it. I first met Margo when I was going through my rounds of full body radiation and high doses of chemotherapy.

Having the double whammy of chemo and radiation wreaks havoc on your body. I was puking all the time. I didn't feel like eating; it *hurt* to eat. I was so tired, my mind wasn't clear, and I got mouth ulcers. It felt as if I were on the verge of death, which I was.

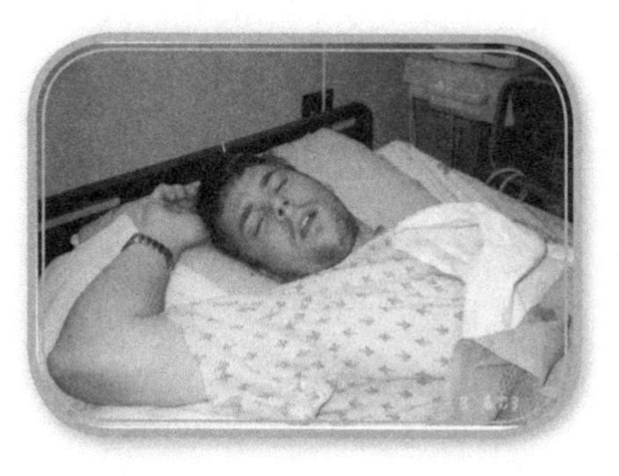

The effects of the radiation and chemo made me sicker than I'd ever been. It felt like I was at the brink of death.

You have to be careful during this critical time; a lot of people end up in the intensive care unit because of infection or sickness caused by a compromised immune system. The goal is that the donor's bone marrow cells will take and a new immune system will form. If the donor cells don't take, you're left without the ability to fight any and all infections.

MAGIC OF THE SMALL THINGS

In life, it's the smallest things that make a big difference. Every time Nurse Margo came through my door, her smile gave me the hope to continue on.

There was a study in *Good Housekeeping* that stated the average four-year old laughs or smiles up to four hundred times a day. How many times have you laughed and smiled today? The sad part of the study is that by the age of thirty, the number drops to fifteen. One of the easiest and most powerful things you can do is to laugh and smile. It's been over ten years since nurse Margo walked through my hospital door and I can still picture her smile; the magic is in the moment.

Below is an acronym I created to help you remember the importance and difference a smile makes:

Small or large
Motivates
Inspires
Lasting impact
Energizes you and others

Even though I was the sickest I had ever been in my life, I was able to experience a moment of happiness thanks to Nurse Margo and making the choice to elevate my attitude. All you have is the here and now, the present. This is why four year olds laugh up to four hundred times a day. They live in the present and experience the magic in the moment. You can do this by the simple act of smiling. Picture the people you come across on a daily basis who are in need of a smile. You can become their Nurse Margo.

The day you receive the transplant is Day Zero, it's like a new birth. It was as if I had just been given a whole new life; I was in infancy. The actual transplant was a little anticlimactic. The donor's bone marrow cells are red and come in a clear bag. The best way I can describe it is like receiving a blood transfusion. The bone marrow cells were inserted into me through an IV connected to a PICC line in my arm. This is a device similar to a port that allows for medicine to be administered and blood to be drawn. The whole procedure took about forty-five minutes to complete.

If a bone marrow transplant is successful, within two or three days the donor's bone marrow cells will begin to form another immune system. Once that happens, the immune system is susceptible to infections because it's brand new. Upon being released from the hospital, I was instructed not to eat any fresh fruits or vegetables because the bacteria could become harmful to my immune system.

I also had to get all of my childhood shots again since they had been wiped out with the removal of my immune system. When I got my childhood shots the nurse only had children's Band-Aids, so I left with a Big Bird Band-Aid.

In *Man's Search for Meaning,* Dr. Victor Frankl recalled thinking about the little things in life, such as taking bus rides, unlocking front doors, and turning on light switches. He also wrote about being "carried away by nature's beauty" when taking a train ride through the mountains where a man draws the attention of the other passengers to a beautiful sunset.

W	4/14	0	***See chemo calculation policy on page three** **TBI 200 Rads BID @ 0800 & 1400** Start Cyclosporine A (CSA) 2.0mg/kg IV q12 hrs continuous infusion (for a total of 4mg/kg/day). (Monitor blood levels hereafter to maintain levels of 250-350ng/ml – note dose adjustments page 3 below.) **Matched Unrelated Donor marrow stem cell infusion.** Premedicate with Hydrocortisone 100mg IV, Tylenol 650 mg po and Benadryl 50mg IV 30 minutes prior to infusion. **Donor stem cells will arrive in pm today. Red cell content will be checked prior to infusion.**
R	4/15	1	IV methotrexate (IVMTX) **$10mg/m^2$** x1 today CMV PCR *(if pos. at any time, check with staff M.D. for treatment immediately)* IVIG 500mg/kg IV tro 6-8hrs.
F	4/16	2	(NO leucovorin rescue) D/C Allopurinol D/C Zofran
Sa	4/17	3	IVMTX $5mg/m^2$ x1 today
Su	4/18	4	Give leucovorin rescue[1] 24 hours after IVMTX
M	4/19	5	----------
T	4/20	6	IVMTX $5mg/m^2$ x1 today
W	4/21	7	Give leucovorin rescue[1] 24 hours after IVMTX IVIG 500mg/kg IV tro 6-8hrs. CMV PCR on blood with A.M. labs
R	4/22	8	----------
F	4/23	9	----------
Sa	4/24	10	----------
Su	2/25	11	----------
M	4/26	12	Give leucovorin rescue[1] 24 hours after IVMTX
T	4/27	13	----------
W	4/28	14	IVIG 500mg/kg IV tro 6-8hrs. CMV PCR on blood with A.M. labs [Change to PO CSA whenever patient can tolerate pills (**oral dose is approx. 2.5x IV dose** – comes in 25mg and 100mg caps)] Start MVI po q day& Folic acid 1mg po q day.
R	4/29	15	----------

2

The plan put together by my doctors for my bone marrow transplant.

The amazing thing is that all this took place while they were prisoners and robbed of their freedom. These innocent men and women were stripped of their humanity and self-dignity, and were treated worse than livestock, yet they were still able to appreciate life's small wonders. When you recognize that you can appreciate life's small wonders, no matter your circumstances, you realize true joy.

Dr. Frankl, who was a psychologist before being imprisoned in the concentration camps, realized that while so much else was taken from him; no one could take away his ability to choose how to see the world. Frankl wrote, "Love is the ultimate and greatest goal to which you can aspire."

MAGIC OF PEACE

Another small thing, that's actually a big thing, is peace of mind: the ability to remain calm in the face of adversity and not give in to fear or worry. It's something that doesn't come to you because you have material things. Peace comes because you have something inside, because your life is in harmony with its purpose and principles.

Peace is in knowing that worry doesn't solve problems. Peace is being able to maintain an inner calm even when you're constantly bombarded by chaos. It's about having a clear conscience and a fulfilled spirit.

Finding peace is important facet in making the choice to "Elevate Your Attitude." One of the biggest breakthroughs in my marathon of cancer was when I able to find peace with the fact that my life was never going to be the same. Once you reach this place, it becomes possible to move on to healing and finding the victory. It allows you to experience the magic in the moment.

By finding peace, I was able to use the diagnosis and journey with cancer as the single greatest transformational experience of my life. Before the cancer, I was like an ordinary caterpillar. The cancer was my cocoon and I emerged from it a beautiful butterfly.

I see life through new eyes; the old pettiness doesn't matter as much. I see the beauty that everyday holds through the colors of blooming flowers, the warmth of the sun, and the greatness of the night sky. I'm truly blessed, and I count myself as one of the lucky ones, to have experienced this thing called cancer. Not because of the cancer itself, but because of the person I have become through finding peace in the midst of a tragic event.

Peace comes from acceptance, realizing that you cannot change the past but instead believing with everything within you that some good can come about. Peace comes when you realize that when you cannot change your circumstances, you must simply make the best out of them. Peace comes from living in the now, letting go of past regrets, worries, and wondering "if only." Peace is living in the present, not anxious with tomorrow and the challenges and problems it may bring.

Finding peace comes when you realize that even out of the most horrific and tragic events can come some of life's greatest moments and learning experiences. It comes from finding that person inside of you that is greater than you ever imagined existed. Finding peace comes when you allow yourself to be transformed, like the mythical Phoenix who rose from the ashes. The story of the Phoenix is one of my favorites Greek myths as it symbolizes rebirth and transformation.

Three Ways For You To Attain Peace

1. Let go:

Don't hold grudges. If you have any emotional baggage, let it go. One thing that has helped me is realizing that people do the best they can with what they have. That doesn't mean what someone did to you was right, it means it's all right for you to move on. In other words, you forgive the person because you no longer allow them to have power over you. The act of forgiveness is for you, not for them. Just because you forgive doesn't mean you validate what they did was right or allow them to do it to you again.

2. Cultivate faith:

The positive attitude we discussed earlier is essential in having faith in the future. Expect the best. Expect that the universe is conspiring on your behalf, not against you. Believe that when you are true to yourself, things will work out for the best.

3. Get real:

Be realistic about your life. Align your expectations with your skills, abilities, and circumstances. Shoot for great heights, but cut yourself some slack. Stop being your own worst critic. Sometimes you come up short. Recognize that the sun will rise again tomorrow.

One last note on peace; at different points in your life, you will have varying levels of it. Maintaining equilibrium, a state where you feel in balance, is a conscious effort. Things may happen to challenge your decision to be at peace, but you can bring yourself back into alignment by asking this question: "Is this something I can control?"

If the answer is yes, ask yourself what you can do about it, and then "Take Action" on that thing.

If the answer is no, why worry about something you cannot control?

Peace cannot be bought for any amount of money, nor is it something anyone else can give you. It's something you attain on your own. It took me a while to find it, but I've decided to hold onto mine. I wouldn't trade the peace I have for anything!

Peace of Mind is the greatest form of wealth.

THE MAGIC OF FOCUS

In order to experience the fullness and magic in the moment, it's important to maintain focus. So often in life we become distracted, and it's easy to do in the "information overload society" we live in. If you don't stay focused it's more difficult to accomplish the results you desire. That's why this is an important component of the choice to "Elevate Your Attitude." Below are some strategies that will help you to stay focused.

First things first: Life can become so hectic that if you don't make your goals a priority, you can reach the end of the day without doing them.

Organize your thoughts: To succeed in life you must have uncluttered thinking. You accomplish this through clarification of your needs, values, and purpose.

Chart your course: What's the outcome you're seeking? Set a plan of how you'll get from here to there.

Undivided attention: You want all of your energy to be used in fulfilling your dream. Limit your exposure to people, things, and environments that sap your energy.

Single purpose: Many people fail because they try to do too many things. Have one definite purpose, and once that is reached, move onto the next.

Eye on the goal: Beware of distractions that will cause you to detour, and if you do, refocus on the goal at hand.

Day by day: Move closer to your dream by taking action every single day.

THE MAGIC OF LOVE

Experiencing the magic in the moment includes embracing one of the most powerful forces in the world: love. This includes the love of life, yourself, and others. When I got into bodybuilding my main focus was the way my body looked. I devoted hours to lifting weights, cardio, planning my diet, and sleep for recovery.

But cancer stripped that away. It took away my top physical shape, stole my hair, and even swelled my body to an unrecognizable form. I laid in my hospital bed feeling the rock hard muscle I had worked so hard to sculpt turn into flab. When I changed my clothes it was painful seeing the fat replacing muscle. It seemed that overnight all of the years of hard work were cancelled out.

I missed the feeling of pumping iron and it was difficult to go from a place of strength to weakness. I had to come to terms with my new reality. I had to figure out if I could love myself on the inside even when I wasn't looking my best on the outside.

I had a choice, and so do you. Sure, you want to be at your top form in every way, including physically. But when you aren't, are you still able to love yourself? Are you still able to embrace your perceived imperfections? Realizing that perfection is in the imperfections, because perfection is being your authentic self. As Dr. Seuss wrote, "Today you are You, this is truer than true. There is no one alive who is Youer than You."

In the end, it doesn't matter how much money you have left in your bank account, if you drove the latest model sports car, or if you lived in a house overlooking the ocean. Success is measured by the love you give and receive. Our relationships with family and friends are the greatest assets we have.

It's unfortunate when we take the people we love the most for granted and fail to appreciate them fully. Sometimes, we treat them less than they deserve because we know they will still love us. Other times we don't tell them how much they really mean to us.

We cannot survive without love; it's priceless and makes life worth living. Without it, the world is colorless. Love gives life its passion, zest, and meaning.

One of my favorite quotes on love comes from Emmet Fox, who said the following:

"There is no difficulty that enough love will not conquer. There is no disease that enough love will not heal. No door that enough love will not open. No gulf that enough love will not bridge. No wall that enough love will not throw down. And if you could love enough you would be the happiest and most powerful person in the world."

To fully experience the magic in the moment, make sure you reward yourself as you reach a goal or an achievement. It's also important to remember to celebrate life as you go along your journey. Don't wait until the end to celebrate life and all it offers. Each day you wake up is a celebration; you've been given the gift of another day! Life is a magical experience filled with wondrous joys and pleasant surprises. Celebrate your life, your family, your friends, your victories, and your future.

Experiencing the magic in the moment is being able to live fully each day. This is one of the greatest gifts I received from having cancer at such a young age. It made me realize how precious every moment of life is. We are here one moment and gone the next. It can be easy to take life for granted and instead of really living it to the fullest, to just go through the motions. None of us knows how long we have on Earth. That is why it is important to live each day realizing what a precious gift it is.

It's easy to get so caught up in the busyness of life that we miss out on living. One way this happens is getting stuck in the trap of moaning and groaning about our circumstances in life. Complaining becomes a downward spiral that keeps us from enjoying the fullness of life. It robs us of the everyday magic that occurs around us.

One night, after giving a talk, a man from Uganda approached me. He shared that in his country the average yearly income is only two hundred and forty six dollars, and that eighty percent of the population has no access to fresh water. I think how often I take for granted a sip of water. For too many people in the world, the basic necessity of water is a luxury. So often the small things are really the big things: a child's laughter, a sip of hot cocoa on a cold wintery day, the warm embrace of a loved one.

Everyday above ground is a good day!

The magic of life is in the moment.

One of the side effects of my chemotherapy was decreased production of healthy white blood cells. This made me more susceptible to getting infections. This meant the all but one of my treatments had to be done as an inpatient. For me that was one of the most challenging things I had to deal with.

Being away from family, friends, and barely having any energy to leave my hospital bed wore on me mentally. It seemed like time stood still, waiting until the day the doctor would release me to go home. It was as if the whole world was progressing and experiencing life, and I was just standing still.

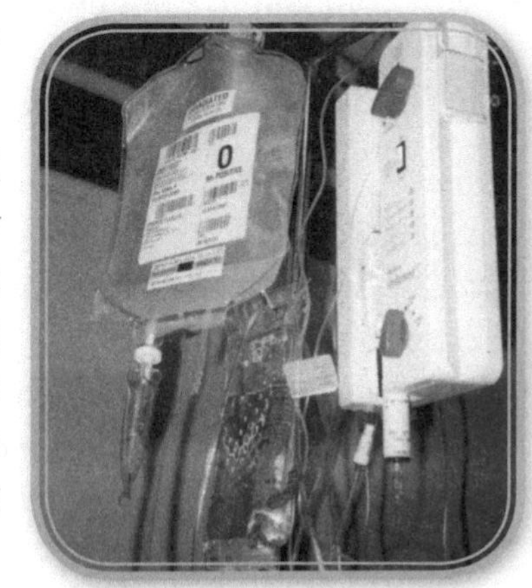

One of the side effects of leukemia is a decrease in the production of platelets requiring a transfusion.

THE MAGIC OF PATIENCE

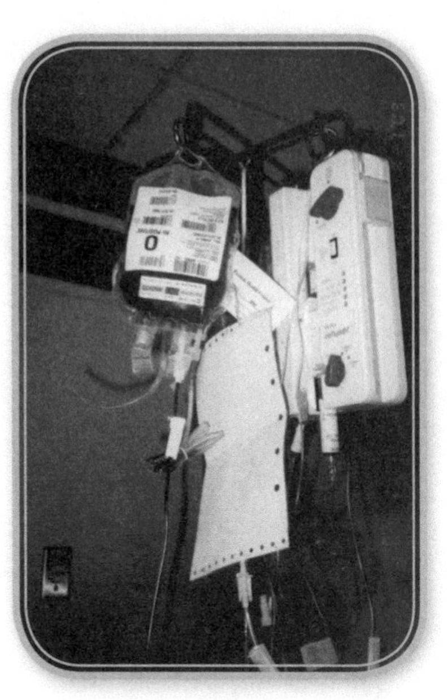

Besides platelet transfusions I also had to receive blood transfusions.

One of the hardest lessons in life is to learn patience. This is especially true in today's society of instant coffee, microwaves, and television on demand. Many people are like the person who prayed, "God give me patience, and give it to me now!" When you are battling adversity or striving to achieve greater victory, developing patience becomes a necessity.

Spending all those days, weeks, and months in the hospital taught me the necessity of practicing patience in order to experience the magic in the moment. I realized that the healing process takes time. You don't become healthy or get back to being normal overnight. Long after the treatments were finished and I was in remission, the process of readjusting back to life was still taking place.

For a long time, I felt lost, and out of place with the rest of the world as I tried to readjust. When you're battling cancer, you think that if only you can get into remission then life will be perfect and you'll have no more problems. I think, in some ways, readjusting to life after cancer is just as difficult as fighting it.

In life, as in overcoming adversity, you have to practice patience. Patience with the doctors, nurses, treatment, loved ones, and most importantly, yourself. Patience is a learned behavior and one of choice. One of the greatest benefits of going through cancer was having the time to be able to examine my life and where it was headed. So often, we get caught up in the hustle and bustle of life that we never take time to know if we are headed in the right direction. When you spend most of your day in a hospital bed, you have plenty of time for personal reflection and focusing on what matters most in life.

When you're experiencing adversity, it's easy to feel overwhelmed and that you don't have control over anything in your life. Worry, doubt, and fear take over your thoughts. This is why it's essential to be joyful. No matter what is happening to us, we can always choose to be joyful. Joy isn't a fleeting emotion that we feel when something good happens to us or everything is perfect. Joy is much deeper than that; it's a lasting attitude that comes through choice.

Joy is not dependent upon your circumstances, but on your attitude.

Being joyful is about finding the good in life. It's living with peace, contentment, and an excitement for life. You find joy in the appreciation of living one more day, time spent in the presence of a loved one, or knowing that there's a greater purpose to all things. By allowing joy to fill my life, I became more powerful than cancer. Joy allowed me to get through relapsing, all the different treatments, and the amount of time it took to recover. The same will be true for you and whatever "character building experience" you face.

The National Speakers Association is the professional association for speakers. At the first national conference I attended, the theme was, "Enjoy the Journey." They even gave out a backpack with that logo on it, and I still have it to this day, because it's such a meaningful message. Becoming successful and reaching your goals doesn't happen overnight. Victory occurs by making the choice of elevating your attitude and experiencing the magic in the moment.

Remember, life is a journey, not a destination, so appreciate the ride. One of the main things that will make your journey magical is the people that accompany you on it. Having cancer made me realize how important my family and friends were. Take this time to reconnect with loved ones and old friends. Tell a spouse, child, parent, or a friend how much you love and appreciate them.

It's important to take time to celebrate life, from the "mundane" to special occasions. What makes my mom so wonderful is that she creates special moments of celebration. I'll never forget my birthday in sixth grade; we went out to eat and she put candles on the pizza like it was a cake. At the time I didn't fully appreciate it and was a little embarrassed. Looking back I realize how blessed I am to have such a wonderful mom.

It was a nice surprise getting off the plane and seeing my family greet me for my 35th birthday.

Even today she still creates special moments of celebration. A few years ago I flew back to Kansas for a talk the day before my birthday. She along with my dad and sister greeted me at the airport and they made a big sign wishing me happy birthday. She also had taped a helium balloon to the sign but it came unattached and when she saw me said, "Matt you're balloon is at the top of ceiling of the airport." A couple of days later when I flew out it was still there, bringing a smile to my face and reminding me how blessed I am for my mother.

One of my favorite songs is, "Celebration," by Kool and the Gang. I love the lyrics, "Celebrate good times, come on!" One of the first times I heard this song was at a theme park as a kid. It played at the end of a magical day. Ever since then that song brings me so much joy when I hear it.

There's so much to celebrate in life. The fact you're reading this right now is cause for celebration. During my marathon with cancer, I learned the importance of celebrating life. Every year I celebrate the day I was diagnosed (September 11th), when I received my bone marrow transplant (April 14th), and the day I left the hospital for good (Mother's Day). One of the greatest days of my life was walking out of the hospital on Mother's Day, 2004. Since then, I have remained in remission.

In life, we celebrate the victory of our favorite sports team and get excited at the concert of our favorite band; why not get excited about your life? I believe one of the most important things is to get excited and celebrate our lives. Right now, think of something you can celebrate, go ahead and throw yourself a party. Life goes by so fast that we often never stop to enjoy it.

What is something that you can celebrate right now?

THE MAGIC OF BEING A HERO

One way you experience the magic in the moment is by creating magical moments for others. One of the reasons why you're reading this right now is because of my bone marrow donor. Without his heroic act of donating marrow, I wouldn't have lived. There would be no more magical moments for me to experience in this life. Before my donor was found two potential matches had been identified, yet for whatever reason they didn't work out.

One of the matches even made it to the workup phase where doctors determine if the donor is healthy enough to give their bone marrow. It was discovered then that they had a life-threating illness and they were able to receive treatment for it. This is another example of a seed of an equivalent or greater benefit.

That was also true in the case of my donor. For one year after your transplant you can have only limited contact with them. The reason for this originated from a situation where the recipient of a bone marrow donation passed away and the donor felt responsible for it. At first, the communication between us consisted only of letters that had any possible identifying personal information blacked out. Receiving letters with sentences blackened out by sharp marker make me thing I was reading material that was top secret.

After a year, I was able to meet my bone marrow donor; his name is Tim Washburn and he is one of my heroes. I'll always be grateful for his simple, yet heroic, act of being a bone marrow donor.

I will always be grateful for my bone marrow donor, Tim. He is a real hero.

Once again, it's an example of how the smallest actions produce the biggest results. Tim was in charge of blood drives for the Red Cross. The first time I met him was when I gave an inspirational/motivational talk to his division; it was a powerful way to share how one of their own saved a life.

Afterward I asked him what made him decide to become a donor. He said that he used to work in sales but after 9/11 he got laid off. This was a national tragedy, and for Tim it was a personal one. He wanted to make a difference, so he went back to school, completed a Masters in Public Health and started working for the Red Cross.

It "just so happened" that the office building where he worked also housed offices for the National Bone Marrow Registry. Tim asked if they would sign up for the blood drive and, being curious, asked what their purpose was. When he found out they saved lives through donations of bone marrow, he immediately signed up. Less than a week later he was contacted to be my donor. People have been on the bone marrow registry list their whole lives; I had been waiting seven months. I learned from Tim that it's not what you do for yourself, but what you do for others, that lasts.

I am a real believer in, and forever grateful for, the National Bone Marrow Donor Program. I encourage everyone to visit the website at www.marrow.org to learn more and consider registering. Being able to give someone the gift of life is one of the greatest gifts you can give. By being a hero you help others experience the magic in the moment.

You become a hero by:

Helping other people

Empathy for other people

Reaching out to other people

Open to serving other people

MAGIC IS IN THE MOMENT

One of the huge turning points in my adventure with cancer was realization that even though I was in the hospital, I could still experience the magic in the moment. This occurred when Ashley's mom came to visit me. Before I got sick, we'd been planning a trip to go see her mom who lived in Key West, Florida. One of my favorite beers is Guinness, which I had in common with her mom and we planned on having one when we visited. All that changed once I was diagnosed and the first time we met was when she came to visit me in the hospital.

Ashley's mom is full of energy and life. She walked through the hospital door with a huge smile on her face and carrying a six-pack of Guinness. However, she'd poured out the beer in the parking lot and filled the bottles with Gatorade. She said that was one of the hardest things she'd ever done. Even though I was in a hospital receiving chemotherapy, we had the time of our lives, laughing and carrying on as if we were hanging out at world famous Sloppy Joe's bar in Key West. At one point, the head nurse came in and was concerned I'd lost my mind. She couldn't understand how someone undergoing treatment for cancer could be having so much fun.

Another time, a nurse came in and said I was laughing too loudly and a patient had complained I was making too much noise. Nurses used to come into my room on their breaks calling it the happiest place in the hospital and referring to it as their oasis. This proves that it's not your circumstances, but your choices, that determine your happiness.

One last way to experience the magic in the moment is to practice savoring. I'm sure, like me, at times you've scarfed down your food, barely even tasting it. In the same way, that's how some people live their lives and, in the process, end up missing out on the magic of the moment. Savoring is making the choice to elevate your attitude by being mindfully aware of the now and fully appreciating what you're now experiencing.

For example, when it comes to food it's enjoying each and every bite of your delicious food and allowing your taste buds to dance with the fullness and richness of your food. Similar to savoring, is my "Freeze-Frame Technique."

This came from the summer before my 6th grade year. I was enjoying a glass of lemonade outside of my house, thinking how wonderful life was and how I wanted to capture the moment. The "Freeze Fame Technique" is about capturing such moments in time.

It when you consciously pause and take a mental picture of the moment. Even though it's has been over twenty-five years, because I captured that moment in my mind, I can close my eyes and go back to that worry free summer, sipping on that glass of ice cold lemonade. Remember to consciously enjoy the moment and the experience you're in. This is when you experience the magic in the moment.

When you make the choice to "Elevate Your Attitude" you're able to experience the magic in the moment.

CHAPTER 9: Ultimate Victory Formula

One of the most important lessons I learned while studying for my PhD in Organizational Leadership was the importance of defining things. Many times you can be saying the same word as someone else and you each have two completely different meanings. I define the concept of attitude as, "The feelings you feel, the thoughts you think, and the words you speak." From this definition I've created what I call the, "Ultimate Victory Formula" and it's also my philosophy for life.

It's as follows: "The feelings you feel, the thoughts you think, and the words you speak, determine the life you live."

Ultimate Victory Formula:
F (Feelings) + T (Thoughts) + W (Words) = L (Life you live)

It was through the "Ultimate Victory Formula" that I was able to go from my darkest days with cancer to creating my brightest future! One of the things I discovered during this process was that my biggest challenge, or "character building experience," wasn't the cancer. The realization that I made was that no matter what challenge you face in life, the biggest one is your own mind: the limiting beliefs, negative self-talk, and the self-defeating inner dialogue.

The "Ultimate Victory Formula" addresses this by focusing on the three things you have control over when you make the choice to "Elevate Your Attitude." They are your feelings, your thoughts, and your words.

FEELINGS YOU FEEL (F)

One of the most important things, and one of the hardest for me to do, while going through my bone marrow transplant was moving my body.

Many times, I was so emotionally and physically drained by the chemotherapy, radiation, and all my various medications that all I wanted to do was to lay in bed.

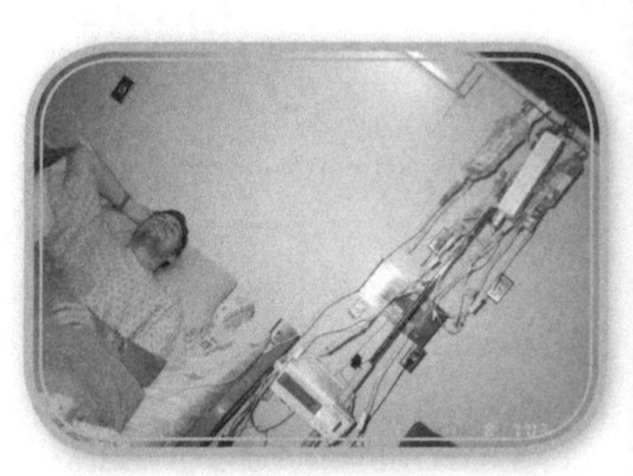

I felt so bad and the last thing I wanted to do was get out of bed.

Dr. Bodensteiner, my main bone marrow transplant doctor, would always get after me to get out of bed. He said if I just walked up and down the hallway of the transplant unit, which was the length of four rooms, I'd be able to get out of the hospital sooner. That was all the motivation I needed. As I shared earlier, by changing your body language you can change your life. By moving your body you produce positive feelings allowing you to "Elevate Your Attitude."

PREFERENCES VERSUS ADDICTIVE DEMANDS

A huge part of how you feel is your emotions. One of the most profound books I've read dealing with emotions is *The Handbook to Higher Consciousness*, by Ken Keyes Jr. The premise is how to control your emotions without your emotions controlling you. Ken was a paraplegic and devoted his life to discovering how to live happily all the time. He believed the answer lies in having preferences versus addictive demands.

According to him, an addictive demand is an emotionally backed thought that says something must be a certain way for you to feel happy, secure, or satisfied. A preference is how you'd like something to be, but if it doesn't turn out that way, you don't get emotionally upset.

For example, my preference when I fly is for my flight to be on time. If it's truly a preference then when my flight gets delayed, it doesn't bother me. I don't get angry, upset, anxious, stressed out, or allow it to cause me to become unhappy.

At times it's been an addictive demand and I've become worried and upset over missing my next flight. I like to think of preferences versus addictive demands in the terms of the old saying, "Don't cry over spilled milk." So often in life, we allow ourselves to become upset over "spilled milk." The milk has already been spilled and you can't change it, so why get upset over it? Too often people give away their power to situations they cannot control or change.

> Daily I have to remind myself to turn my addictive demands into preferences.

Another thing that I learned from Ken Keyes Jr. was the importance of living in the here and now, instead of the dead past or the imagined future. In another one of his books he provides a great example with a cartoon of a couple in a van. They're running out of gas and it shows the woman thinking about yelling at the man, "What do you mean, you forgot to put gas in the car?" The man in the example is thinking ahead and worrying of how he is going to have to walk in the heat of the day to the gas station.

The woman is living in the dead past and the man is living in the imagined future. The next page shows a picture of the two living in the here and now, enjoying each other's company, even though they're still running out of gas.

Both examples are the same circumstance; the difference is how they choose to perceive it. The first is an example of addictive demands and the second is an example of preferences. You have a choice of the emotions you feel, but it's easy to get caught up and expend our energy in things that have already happened, or have not yet happened.

A great example of this for me was with my cancer adventure. When I was first diagnosed and replayed the words "I have cancer" over and over it my head. I was living in the dead past. That was something I couldn't change, so why waste my energy stressing out over it? In psychology it's called rumination, which is compulsively replaying in one's mind a negative event or source of distress. The focus is stuck on the bad feelings and experiences that are rooted in the past. This is contrasted with worry, which is focusing on possible bad events that may occur in the future. Personal examples for me included worrying about relapsing and also the outcome of my future bone marrow transplant.

To live a happier and more fulfilled life, turn addictive demands into preferences.

24-HOUR RULE

One strategy that has been helpful in managing my feelings is something I learned from Don Shula, legendary coach of the Miami Dolphins. He had a "Twenty-Four Hour Rule."

If his team won a game, they could celebrate as much as they wanted for twenty-four hours, but after that, it was time to move on. The same was true for a defeat. For twenty-four hours, they could be down in the dumps about the loss, but then it was time to move on to the next game. This is a great concept to use in life.

In the speaking business, there's the saying, "You're only as good as your last talk." I might give the speech of a lifetime one evening, but when I face my next audience, it doesn't matter how good my last speech was. The same is true on the rare night, that for whatever reason, my talk falls flat. It would be easy to let this discourage me and make me think I'm a failure as a speaker. Applying Don Shula's rule for his players helped me realize that whether it's failure or success, you must move beyond the dead past.

Many people are not willing to move beyond their pasts and get stuck there forever. Others hold onto guilt, shame, and regret. Don't beat yourself up over the past; it's gone forever. Instead, move on with your life and learn from past mistakes. Once again I want to share with you one of Christian Larson's affirmations, "I forget about the mistakes of the past and press on to the greater success of the future."

How do you move beyond the past? Forgive yourself and forgive others. Let go of any grudges. Release it by deciding not to hang on to the past anymore. Create greater successes by climbing higher mountains. Work toward greater achievements and experiencing new things. Always strive to reinvent yourself through constant growth and personal development.

Besides being stuck in the dead past, the worry of the imagined future can keep you from living a victorious life. Worry becomes a personal adversity gremlin. One of the biggest challenges I had to conquer in facing cancer was the worry. Even when you're in remission, the worry is still there. Thoughts such as, "Will it come back?" or "Can I readjust to life?" flood your mind. Perhaps you can never fully rid yourself of worry and to a small degree that's a good thing, because it can be beneficial. Early detection and prevention are two of the most important factors in conquering cancer. Worry can provide feedback that certain action needs to be taken.

However, most of the things you worry about never happen and are out of your control. Therefore, it does no good stressing about most of things you worry about daily. As you know, this is easier said than done. The most effective way not to worry is to occupy your mind with something else.

Below are some helpful suggestions to eliminate worry.

Enjoy Life
Love and Be Loved
Imagine Being Healthy
Meditate
Inspire Others
Never Give Up Hope
Appreciate the Small Things
Treat Yourself
Envision a Brighter Future

Wish Upon a Star
Open your Heart to the Good in Life
Reflect on Good Times
Remember All the Positive Things in Your Life
You are More Powerful than Any Adversity

Worry is one of the biggest quenchers of passion. Being from Kansas, one of my favorite movies is *The Wizard of Oz*. In my talks I share what I call the "Tin Man Syndrome." If you remember from the movie when Dorothy, Toto, and the Scarecrow met the Tin Man, he couldn't move. He got stuck in a thunderstorm without his oilcan and became rusted. Too many people are like that: rusted, stuck in a rut, and going through the motions. They've been caught out in the storm of life and like the Tin Man, who needed his oil can, they are in need of an infusion of passion. They go through life like zombies, dead men and women walking.

People just going through the motions remind me of the words of Benjamin Franklin, "Many people die at twenty-five and aren't buried until they are seventy-five."

Tin Man Syndrome: "The majority of people are rusted, stuck in a rut, going through the motions. They have been caught out in the storm of life and like the Tin Man, who needed his oil can, they are in need of an infusion of passion in their life."

Passion is the key. When Dorothy is in Kansas, the movie is in black and white. It paints the picture of a dreary and dreadful existence; this all changes when Dorothy lands in Oz and the movie turns to color. In Oz the movie takes on a new vibrancy.

I like to run up from the back of the room after I am introduced to help fire up the audience.

This illustrates how passion can transform your life from a dreary, dreadful, and desperate existence to one that is full, alive, colorful, and vivid. Are you a person full of passion, or are you like the Tin-Man, rusted by the storms of life and stuck in a rut? Do you greet each day with joy and happiness, or dread waking up in the morning? Are you the type of person who says, "Good morning God," or "Good God, it's morning?" Life is precious and full of vibrant color, but too often we allow ourselves to be stuck in a world without color.

Ralph Waldo Emerson said, "Nothing great was ever achieved without enthusiasm." Is there an excitement within you about the service or product you offer? Do you have a burning desire to reach your goals and be the very best you? Too many are just going through the motions, working just enough not to get fired and making just enough not to quit. I encourage you to be among the few that are passionate about what you're doing!

To stay motivated in life, you need to be full of passion. Passion gives you the energy to work late and rise early in the morning. It allows you to continue pursuing your goal instead of quitting. Passion overcomes fear and worry so you can stay the course.

One of the benefits of having cancer was that it gave me a greater passion for life. The good news is that you don't need to have a terminal illness to create more passion in your life. Passion is what creates a champion in the soul of an ordinary person.

To create more passion in life, remember the ABC's of passion: Appreciation, Blessing, and Contentment.

THE ABC'S OF PASSION:

Appreciation: Often it takes losing something or someone before we fully appreciate what we had; after cancer I had a greater appreciation for my health because I lost it for a time. On a smaller scale, maybe you've experienced this with a cold. When you're sniffling and aching, when your head is hurting or your eyes watering, you suddenly miss the days of feeling well. Your health takes on a new meaning.

Picture how many times you have taken for granted when you walk into the room, flip the light switch, and the light turns on. Think how much of a luxury air-conditioning is on a hot sweltering day or having a heater to stay warm on an unbearably freezing day. Yet many times it can be easy for us not to fully appreciate these blessings.

Appreciation reminds you how good your life is. It's also important to be appreciative of the people in your life. I'm so appreciative for my doctors (even Dr. Doom), nurses, and all the healthcare professionals who helped save my life.

Blessings: Passion is also about counting the blessings in life. It's important to do this every day. It's so easy to focus on what's going wrong in life; instead, focus on what's right. For instance, you might complain that your alarm didn't go off (or you hit snooze too many times) so you got out of bed late. You grumble all the way out of the driveway and onto the freeway until you see the accident being cleared away just ahead of you on the road. Suddenly, the fact that you were late may have been a blessing: perhaps it saved you from another fate.

One of the challenges of dealing with adversity is being able to find the blessings in your life. It's easy to focus on the negative things that are happening to you. When I was dealing with my "character building experience" of cancer I would think about my friends on the weekend having a good time while I was stuck in a hospital bed. Things began to turn around for me when I started to look for the blessings that were in my life.

Some of these blessings were knowledgeable doctors, nurses that cared, love of family and friends, and the belief that this experience would make me a better person. When I was a kid one of the songs I remembering singing in church contained the words, "Count your blessings, name them one by one." Those are good words to live by. There are so many blessings around us; I've come to believe that cancer was one of the greatest blessings in my life.

Contentment: Are you fulfilled? It's easy to get caught in the trap of thinking you need something or someone else to make you content. True fulfillment and contentment comes from the inside; it's a conscious choice. It's about choosing to have a positive feeling where you're at right now. This doesn't mean you shouldn't desire more, or aspire to improve yourself. It means that true contentment comes from the inside, knowing you are doing the best you can with what you have and also recognizing the need to grow daily.

You may know someone who is waiting for their knight in shining armor, or to win the lottery. They say, "If only ________________ would happen, then I'd be happy." But when you're constantly searching for something outside of you for fulfillment, you'll never find real contentment. When you look for happiness outside of yourself, you only end up with a mirage. You can experience true passion today, no matter what your external circumstances are, because you're joyous on the inside. It's a choice; eventually I learned how to find contentment while battling cancer because I realized it wasn't dependent upon my circumstances.

A great example of living with passion is John Wesley who was a famous traveling preacher in the 1700's. People came by the masses to hear him. When asked why so many people came to hear him, he replied, "When you set yourself on fire, people love to come and see you burn." Do you have a fire about you when it comes to life? Realizing you're in control of your feelings allows you to "Elevate Your Attitude."

I'm irrationally passionate about sharing my story and message.

THOUGHTS YOU THINK (T)

The second part of the "Ultimate Victory Formula" and the choice to "Elevate Your Attitude" is mastering your thoughts. The only thing that really stands between where you are now and achieving greater victory is YOU! It's your limiting beliefs, negative self-talk, and self-defeating inner conversations that will rob you of your motivation to succeed. At times in our life we create our own self-imposed adversity. Once again I call these your "Thought Gremlins."

Instead of feeding them, causing havoc and the destruction of achieving greater victory in your life; focus on thoughts that come from an ancient truth: "Whatever is true, whatever is noble, whatever is right, whatever is pure, whatever is lovely, whatever is admirable, if anything is excellent or praiseworthy, think on these things."

What kinds of thoughts do you allow into your mind on a daily basis? What TV shows and movies do you watch? What are the lyrics and message of the music you listen to? How about the conversations you have? Do they empower you or do they feed the "Thought Gremlins" within? Just as you can only get out of your refrigerator what you put into it, the same is true for your mind.

"A word fitly spoken is like apples of gold in settings of silver."

The most crucial thing that you must do every single day is to "Elevate Your Attitude." You must turn an attitude of defeat into one of victory and an attitude of negativity into one of possibility; you must adopt an attitude of perseverance and expectancy.

Elevating your attitude is a daily necessity. The first step is realizing that it's possible. If someone else has done it, you can do it too. I knew it was possible to run a marathon because older and less athletic people than me had done it.

Second, you must realize that to "Elevate Your Attitude" is a daily choice. You cannot always control what happens to you. The one thing you always have control over is your own attitude; and sometimes this requires you to talk back to that negative inner voice or as I call it your "Inner Dr. Doom."

At the starting line of my first marathon that voice said to me, "Matt you can't do this, only one-tenth of one percent of the world as ever completed a marathon. You have had cancer, still on medication, and one year removed from chemotherapy. There is no way you can finish, save yourself the embarrassment, and quit now." By making the choice to elevate my attitude I told it two words: "Hush Up!"

Many times we are our own Dr. Doom, holding ourselves back with limiting beliefs, negative self-talk, and self-defeating inner dialogue. A powerful breakthrough is when you recognize that you are not your thoughts. When you go to a buffet you have all these food choices, but just because you see it doesn't mean you have to put it on your plate. Even if you put it on your plate that doesn't mean you have to eat it.

Just because you think something doesn't mean you have to accept it, it doesn't mean it's true. Just like you choose what to eat at a buffet, you can choose the thoughts you accept. You have the choice to accept them, or to reject them.

Another powerful strategy you can use when it comes to your thoughts is a concept I created called "StopThink." This is the process of interrupting limiting beliefs, negative self-talk, and self-defeating thoughts. You practice it by saying "cancel, cancel, cancel" and repeating a victory affirmation when you have a limiting belief, negative self-talk, or a self-defeating thought.

An exam example of "StopThink" is when you are driving and someone cuts you off in traffic and you get that thought of what an idiot they are and begin to get upset. You practice "StopThink" by repeating the words, "cancel, cancel, cancel" and say, "I'm too blessed to be stressed."

Remember these words by Wayne Dyer, "You cannot always control what goes on outside, but you can always control what goes on inside."

You are not your thoughts!

WORDS YOU SPEAK

The last part of the "Ultimate Victory Formula" and this is huge, are the words you speak. As I shared earlier, "There is life and death in the power of the tongue." One of the most powerful things you can do to overcome adversity and achieve greater victory is to speak words of life. As a child you may have said the following phrase, "Sticks and stones may break my bones, but words will never hurt me."

Yet words do hurt, and when it comes to conquering your challenges to achieve greater victory they can become the difference between life and death. This was true for me in conquering cancer. The words you speak and the thoughts you think determine your emotions. Positive emotions aid in the healing process, whereas negative ones hinder it.

That first night in the hospital, when I was repeating over and over, "I have cancer," I was speaking words of death to myself. There's power in the spoken word and the thoughts we think. The words you speak and the thoughts you think attract the life you live.

Three Ways For You To Speak Words of Life

1. DO NOT OWN YOUR ADVERSITY

One thing I made sure to do was to never say "my cancer." That's giving power to it. When I'm referring to the cancer, instead of saying "my cancer," I always say "the cancer."

2. MONITOR YOUR SELF-TALK

Self-talk is what we say or think to ourselves. Researchers estimate that eighty percent of the thoughts an average person thinks are negative. You can combat negative self-talk through affirmations. Here are three you can use:

— It's Great to be Alive!

— I am More POWERFUL than _________(insert your "character building experience")!

— Every day, in every way, I'm getting better and better!

3. HAVE PEOPLE SPEAK WORDS OF LIFE TO YOU

As I mentioned earlier, when my friend Justin said there were over ten million cancer survivors and I could be one as well, those were words of life. You cannot afford to be around people who speak words of death, including doctors.

BEETLE BAILEY EFFECT

As a child one of my favorite things was reading the Sunday comics. I always made sure to read Beetle Bailey. If you're familiar with this comic you know that the main character, Beetle Bailey, was a private in the Army. The other main character was Sarge who was always getting after Beetle Bailey for not doing his job. Sarge would catch Beetle Bailey sleeping, slacking off, and making some kind of excuse to get out of work.

One of the things I share in my leadership talks and trainings is what I call the "Beetle Bailey Effect." People will rise or fall based on the expectations you have of them. Sarge expected Beetle Bailey to slack off, and he did. This is why it's so important to speak words of life to people.

I'm so thankful for Dr. McNamara and Nurse Ginger who set into my mind the expectation that I could get through my adversity of cancer, and it could become a blessing. I shudder, even now, thinking what might have been if Dr. Doom had been my first doctor and set the expectation for my adventure with cancer.

Research has found that the majority of people in prison were told as a child, "One day, you'll end up in jail." The children fulfilled the expectation that was set of them. This is known as the golem effect, which occurs when people are given low expectations and they lower their behavior to match them. The effect is named after a clay creature from Jewish mythology.

Another example of expectations effecting behavior was a study involving teachers who were told that certain students in their classroom could be expected to perform better than others due to be intelligently superior. The reality was that all the students were on a similar intellectual level.

The expectation of the teachers became a self-fulfilling prophecy, as the children that were identified as being more intellectual showed achievement by the end the school year. The researchers conducting the study attribute the development in the students to more attention given to them by the teacher based on the expectation that they were more intelligent.

This is known in psychology as the Pygmalion effect. It occurs when a greater expectation is placed upon a person and they live up to it. The effect is named after the Greek myth of Pygmalion who fell in love with a statue he had carved of a woman.

The "Beatle Bailey Effect" is also important to use in your self-talk. One of my affirmations when going through my cancer experience was, "I am more POWERFUL than cancer!" That's why it's important to "Visualize Your Victory." It becomes a self-fulfilling prophecy.

Speak words of life to yourself and others.

Words themselves are neutral, neither negative nor positive; they're just a collection of letters or characters. What gives words their power is the emotional meaning you give them. You choose the emotional feelings that words create inside of you. It's not just the word itself, other factors such as the content, tone, situation, and especially the person using them affects the meaning of the word.

When it comes to achieving greater victory and overcoming adversity you want to use words that emotionally empower you. There are two ways you can do this. First, change the emotional meaning behind the word or the second way, which is easier, is for you to change the word.

This is why I call myself a cancer conqueror instead of a cancer survivor, and also why I always refer to cancer as the cancer and never my cancer. I didn't want to claim ownership of it. Once again, there is life and death in the power of the tongue. In this negative society we live in, so many people speak words of death versus ones of life.

A great example of this is something I heard while listing to the legendary motivational speaker Zig Ziglar during "Automobile University." He was talking about an alarm clock. I'm sure, like me, you don't get warm fuzzies when you hear or think of the word alarm. Zig suggested, instead of calling it an alarm clock, call it an opportunity clock. I like to call it a "Victory Clock." You think about it, every day your "Victory Clock" goes off is another day you're alive, another opportunity to achieve your dreams, and make a difference in the life of someone else.

I was giving a keynote to an association of bill collectors and told them that I don't believe in bills. They all gave me looks and one woman said, "I'm coming after you to collect!" Then I explained that they aren't "bills," they're "blessings!" Paying the electricity bill to have light, the ability to use a computer, or cook, is a blessing.

Whether it's a blessing or a bill; is your choice. When I think of it as a blessing it puts me into an empowered and happy state. Before, when I saw bills as bills, I remember how getting a single letter in the mail could bring me down. An example of this was my first bill from the hospital, but it was actually a blessing, one that saved my life.

Two more examples of words that cause negative emotions are "work" and "job." This goes as far back as the story of the Garden of Eden, found in The Bible, when Adam is cursed to work the land. A personal example of this happened while I was sitting in a coffee shop on a Saturday, "working" on this book, when a gentleman sat down next to me and saw that I was on my computer. He commented, "Eww, working on the weekend. I'm going to try to hold off until Monday." I thought to myself, "This isn't work, for me, it's play and creation."

When people ask me what I do for work I reply, "I don't work, I play and create!" Thinking of work doesn't get me excited or motivated. However, I love to create and play all day and all nightlong. Once again the take away, is recognizing the emotional power beyond words and how it is easier to change the word versus the motional meaning a word has.

Sometimes, after a talk, I'm asked, "What do you like to do for fun?" I tell them, what I just did! Traveling around the country sharing my story and inspiring others is play for me. It gets me fired up, pumped up, and inspired; I get jazzed! Writing this book, knowing that it's going to make a difference in your life, is play for me.

Here's an important point; just because I call it play instead of work doesn't mean I'm not still putting massive amounts of effort into it. Viewing it as play makes it more enjoyable, I'm more productive, and I put in more effort than when I view it as work! Back in my bodybuilding days, when I was doing multiple sets of leg presses equal to thousands of pounds, exerting massive amounts of effort, sweating, and grunting the weight up the sled, someone said, “Wow, you’re really working hard!” My reply was, “I’m just playing!”

It’s always my pleasure and honor to sign copies of books after my talks.

It’s all a mindset; when you love what you do, it becomes play! In my talks, I share that if all you’re doing is picking up a paycheck, you need a new profession. But I realize that sometimes you feel stuck in a situation where it’s hard to see work as play.

Let me give you an example of such a situation that I experienced; in order to help pay my way through college, I was “working” at a factory. One of the toughest and most dreaded jobs was being an order-filler. This consisted of running the length of the warehouse approximately the size of two football fields. The warehouse was built on concrete and got extremely hot during the summer and freezing cold in the winter. The job was to carry heavy boxes filled with baked goods to the semi-trailers for shipment. Shifts would last ten to twelve hours, sometimes longer.

In order to keep my sanity, I had to turn it into a game; every shift I tried to beat my high score, loading more goods on the truck than I did before. Another strategy to turn work into play is to find the purpose in it. Working at the factory was the means to a greater end: achieving a college degree.

One day, I met an elderly gentleman who had worked at the factory for over twenty years; the job was also play for him. His purpose was providing a better life for his family. Instead of asking people, “How was work?” I like to ask them, “How was play?” As kids we play doctor, house, or in my case I played church and was the preacher. Why does that have to stop?

Another example with the word work occurred after one of my talks when a gentleman was sharing how his son didn’t like doing his homework. My favorite class was recess so I could identify; I suggested to him instead of calling it homework to call it “homeplay.” Once again, it’s not the word, but the emotional meaning you give to the word. The same is true for the word job. I would suggest, instead of calling it your job, call it your “service.” Ultimately every job, in some way, serves someone else. Dr. Albert Schweitzer said, “The purpose of human life is to serve, and to show compassion and the will to help others.” By looking at your work and job as play and service, you can turn your alarm clock into your “Victory Clock.”

MOTHER’S DAY VICTORY

On Mother’s Day 2004, I’d been in the hospital for one month; it was my personal deadline to be out. For the most part it had gone smoothly with my transplant, and my body had accepted the bone marrow from Tim.

However, my lab results weren’t at the level my doctors had hoped. In order for me to be released they would have to improve, which could be two or more days. I was so ready to get out of the hospital. Being confined to the bone marrow unit had taken its toll on me.

The doctor on duty that day was Dr. Ganguly, and upon entering my room he said, “Matt, are you ready to go home?” It was like winning the lottery! I pinched myself to make sure I wasn’t dreaming. My labs that morning unexpectedly rebounded and were good enough for me to leave. The first thing I did was call my mom. Excitedly I said, “Happy Mother’s Day, I get to come home!” My mom said it was the greatest Mother’s Day gift ever.

Before leaving, a nurse brought me slips of paper from the doctor. At first I thought they were gift certificates for having made it through such a long and hard ordeal. They were actually prescriptions for all the medications I would be on. I would have to take close to twenty-five pills a day for several years!

As I walked out of KU Med Center on Mother's Day 2004, back in remission after a successful bone marrow transplant, I thought back to September 11, 2002 when I first walked through the doors of St. Francis Hospital. I'd gone through hell and back. Never in my wildest dreams, or should I say nightmares, could I have imagined all that I would endure. If you would've told me then what I would experience, I would've said there is no way I could have made it. The fact that I walked out of that hospital is proof that you can walk out of whatever adverse situation your experiencing.

Sharing the story of receiving my life changing phone call.

When I got the go-ahead to leave, it was like I was stretching my wings for the first time. When I got to step out of the hospital, I took in all the sights and sounds. Victory felt so good. My first destination was the Wendy's drive-thru. I got a chocolate Frosty, fries, and a bacon cheeseburger. I felt so blessed to be closing this chapter of my life.

However, my journey was just beginning. I had conquered cancer three times; and for close to two years, survival had been my entire focus. Now what? This would ultimately entail two things and take me back to the original victory I was visualizing when first diagnosed. That some good, some how, somewhere, and for someone, would come from this. This would lead me on my journey to become a life changing inspirational and motivational leadership speaker. My other journey was to complete my first marathon. The recovery was slow; many times I fell and still do to this day.

Once again it doesn't matter how many times you fall, as long as you get back up! Knocked down, but never knocked out! When I come up short or feel like quitting, the words of my dad always echo in my mind, "You can do it Matt, one step at a time, you can do it son."

As a precaution for the cancer in my cerebral spinal fluid, I was scheduled to receive ten rounds of chemotherapy stretched over the course of a year. This was to be administered via spinal tap, a very dangerous procedure because inserting the needle in the wrong spot can cause paralysis, or even death. My final one was scheduled for June of 2005.

The lab results always came back clean, but I was concerned about the possible side effects of receiving chemo in my brain. I joked, "I need all the brain cells I can get." Before the last spinal tap, I asked my doctor, "Do I really need this last chemo treatment? I mean, what does the medical literature say?" When I heard his answer, it became crystal clear that I needed to share my story. He said, "Matt, there is no medical literature. There has never been someone who had what you had, who's been alive a year later."

I stood there in complete shock, realizing the impossible odds I'd had overcome, recognizing the insurmountable victory that had occurred. Sometimes I wonder, "Why me? Why am I so blessed to have woken up this morning?" The reason why I'm here is the reason why you're here. You have a special and unique purpose that only **you** can fulfill!

SAN DIEGO ROCK 'N' ROLL MARATHON

In June 2006, after my one-year anniversary of finishing chemotherapy, I stood among twenty-two thousand people waiting for the starting gun to fire at the San Diego Rock 'N' Roll Marathon! Standing there, anticipating the 26.2 miles ahead, a little voice in the back of my head spoke up. "Matt, what are you doing here? Only one-tenth of one percent of the world's population has ever completed a marathon. You've had cancer and are still on medication. There's no way you can finish. It's not possible!" Thinking back on everything I'd overcome I knew that it was possible for me to finish. Just like it's possible for you to overcome the challenges you face and achieve greater victory both personally and professionally in your life.

I told that little voice of limiting beliefs, negative self-talk, and self-defeating inner dialogue two words: "Hush Up!"

I had gone from being a three-time cancer conqueror, having to relearn how to walk, and going through a bone marrow transplant, to now getting ready to fulfill my victory of running a marathon!

I had to pinch myself to make sure I wasn't dreaming. Over the loud speaker, my favorite, song "Beautiful Day" by U2, played. After that the National Anthem played as I got goose bumps; I'd done it. I couldn't believe that a year ago, I was lying face down on an operating table receiving chemotherapy. Now I was getting ready to run 26.2 miles. Images of my dad pushing me around the hospital in a wheelchair and tying my shoes flooded my mind.

I have been asked which was harder, "running a marathon or going through cancer." My reply is the marathon because with cancer I just had to lie in bed.

Bang, the starting gun fired, and off we went. Over the next twenty-six miles I reflected on the roller coaster ride of the last few years. It was such a great feeling coming down that final stretch. I had gone twenty-six miles, and I never realized how far .2 miles could be.

The spectators were cheering as I came down the final stretch, "You can do it, no problem, piece of cake," they shouted! I thought to myself, "Easy for them to say, they had been sitting in the bleachers all day!" My mom and dad flew in from Kansas to see me achieve my victory and cross the finish line.

Upon crossing the finish line, I put my arms up in the victory pose. A volunteer from the race came up and hung a medal around my neck. Even though I finished something like eighteen thousand one hundred and fifty ninth, it was like I received an Olympic gold medal!

Crossing that finish line would've never been possible if I didn't make the choice to visualize my victory of running a marathon, if I didn't make the choice to "Take Action" by taking that first step, and if I didn't make the choice to elevate my attitude. The fact that I was able to conqueror cancer three times, relearn how to walk, go through a bone marrow transplant, and run marathons around the world is great news for you. Because like me, if you make the same three choices I made, you can transcend your adversity and cross your finish line of the victory you want to achieve. By making the choice to "Visualize Your Victory," to "Take Action," and to "Elevate Your Attitude" you develop your "Marathon Mentality."

YOUR ULTIMATE VICTORY

While I was recovering from my bone marrow transplant, I came across a powerful life-changing book, called *The Alchemist*. It's by Paulo Coelho and is the story of a young shepherd boy named Santiago. He had a dream about buried treasure and left everything he knew behind to set out on a journey to find it. He went to new lands and experienced numerous adventures and setbacks. When it seemed that all hope was lost, he found the treasure in the most unexpected of places.

At the end, he realized his dream and his Personal Legend. Coelho defines Personal Legend as a person's deepest desire, or purpose, in his or her life. Just like Santiago found his Personal Legend, you have one too. You have a special and unique legend that only you can fulfill. Earlier in the book, I shared how I ask people to hold out their index finger and share how just like you have a unique fingerprint, you have a unique purpose that only you can fulfill. This is the ultimate lesson I took away from the tale of Santiago in *The Alchemist.*

The Alchemist is inspiring because it's the tale of a young man who realized what so many people don't. He was willing to sacrifice it all to find and live his true purpose in life. Too often, this isn't the case and people settle for less than what their lives could be. I know this isn't true of you, because you're taking the time to read this book. You are one of the few who, like Santiago, want to live out your Personal Legend, your special purpose in life.

The greatest blessing of having cancer is the opportunity to inspire others through my story.

Getting cancer served as a turning point; I've been transformed and now I see the world with new eyes. Facing death is a definite way to alter your perception on life; everything else pales in comparison. However, you don't have to face death to gain a new perspective, or realize the difference your attitude makes on the life you live.

Today I echo the words nurse Ginger shared, "Getting cancer has been one of the greatest blessings of my life." Though I have reminders: scars on my body, pinwheels in my eye because of the infection in my brain, bones weakened by radiation, and not being able to have my own children; I took tragedy and turned it into triumph. You can do the same. All I did was make the three simple choices you have learned about in this book.

Today I am blessed to be able to travel the world, offering inspiration and hope to others through my story of overcoming adversity. One of the main things I hope you take away from this book is that when it comes to your victory it's not the outside stuff that matters, but the inside stuff that counts. That by developing your "Marathon Mentality" through making the choice to "Visualize Your Victory," "Take Action," and "Elevate Your Attitude," it's possible to cross whatever finish line *you* choose. As you cross the finish line remember to hold your hands high above you and yell, **"VICTORY, VICTORY, VICTORY!"**

Epilogue

One of my first professional talks was at Alice Lloyd College, which is nestled away in the picturesque Appalachian Mountains in Kentucky. The college has streets named the Propose Road, Perseverance Lane, and Courage Drive. It is based on the Purpose Road Philosophy. This consists of the use of one's unique talents and gifts to live a life of worldwide service.

One last thought I would like to share, and the most important choice I learned in my adventure with adversity from cancer is making the choice to "Serve Others." This is what I call the "Ultimate Choice." Dr. Albert Schweitzer said, "I don't know what your destiny will be, but one thing I know: the only ones among you who will be really happy are those who will have sought and found how to serve."

Once again you have a unique and special purpose. You have talents and gifts that only you have to offer the world. The ultimate choice is to choose to use them to serve others.

True success is living a life of significance. This is your ultimate victory and it happens when you give back to humanity and make the world a better place because you were born. What will you be remembered for? What mark will you leave behind? To live life of significance, you must be wiling to serve others. It's about being able to transcend your "character building experiences" and helping others to do the same for theirs.

My biggest victory in life has been taking the tragedy of cancer and turning it into triumph by sharing my story with others. It has allowed me to live a life of significance. Remember, out of your mess comes your message; out of your test comes your testimony.

What will your contribution be? Remember, what you do for yourself fades away, but what you do for others lasts. Join me in going beyond a life of success for just yourself and live a live of significance for others. Together you and I can help others achieve greater VICTORY!

GLOSSARY OF VICTORY TERMS

ACT: **A**bsolute **C**ontrol of **T**houghts

Action Based Goal: Goals where you have almost one hundred percent control in completing them. This is in contrast with result-based goals, which are outside of your control if you complete them.

Action Cycle: Process of taking action that consists of the following three parts: take action, get feedback, and make adjustments and start the three-part process over again.

Action Loop: The process of beginning and closing an action.

Addictive Demand: Emotionally backed thought that says something must be a certain way for you to feel happy, secure, or satisfied.

Adversity Principle: The process of growing stronger by going through challenges or adversity. Or as I like to call them, character building experiences.

Automobile University: Listening to educational, empowering, and instructional audio programs while in your automobile.

Beetle Bailey Effect: Based off the cartoon Beetle Bailey and the phenomena of people rising or falling based on your expectation of them.

Character Building Experience: A more empowering way to say and think about challenges.

Create and Play: Words with a positive feeling and emotion used to replace the word work.

Don't Give Away Your Chip: Process of not giving away or up on a victory you want to achieve.

Energy Vampires: Negative people who suck the energy out of you.

FEAR: **F**alse **E**vidence **A**ppearing **R**eal.

FLOSS: Daily personal mastery activities that help rid your mind of negativity plaque and achieve greater victory in your life. They consist of **F**inding the blessing, **L**istening, **O**pen to learning, **St**art and ending you day by reading, and **S**aying affirmations.

Freeze Frame Technique: The process of when you consciously pause and take a mental picture of the moment your experiencing in order for you to recall that moment at a future time.

HERO: Helping other people, **E**mpathy for other people, **R**eaching out to other people, **O**pen to serving other people

Information Overload Society: Term used to describe the massive amount of information a person is bombarded with on a daily basis. It can lead to paralysis by analysis.

Law of Momentum: Objects in motion tend to stay in motion.

Leapfrog Action Strategy to Success: Using the experience of others to reduce your learning curve.

Magic is in the Moment: Process of experiencing the present by being fully in the here and now.

Make No Your Vitamin: The practice of getting excited over hearing the word no because you realize every no you hear is one step closer to a yes.

Marathon Mentality: Mindset to push through the walls of negativity, setbacks, and obstacles to cross your finish line and achieve your victory.

Massive Action Principle: The smallest actions produce the biggest results.

Negativity Plaque: The buildup of limiting beliefs, self-defeating inner dialogue, and self –defeating thoughts in your mind.

Preference: How you'd like something to be, but if it doesn't turn out that way, you don't get emotionally upset.

Posttraumatic Growth: The psychological positive benefits gained from going through a traumatic event. Also known as PTG.

REACT: Responding **E**motionally to **A**ddictive **C**ontrolling **T**houghts

SMILE: Small or Large, **M**otives, **I**nspires, **L**asting impact, **E**nergizes you and others.

Solutionist: Someone who is solution oriented versus problem focused. They ask the question, "What's the solution."

StopThink: This is the process of interrupting limiting beliefs, negative self-talk, and self-defeating thoughts. You practice it by saying "cancel, cancel, cancel" and repeating a victory affirmation when you have a limiting belief, negative self-talk, or a self-defeating thought.

Thought Gremlins: Thoughts consisting of guilt, regret, envy, malice, loathing, irritability, negativity, and scarcity. These thoughts are one reason why a person reacts, versus acts, and operates from addictive demands versus preferences.

Tin-Man Syndrome: The majority of people are rusted, stuck in a rut, going through the motions. They have been caught out in the storm of life and like the Tin Man, who needed his oil can, they are in need of an infusion of passion in their life.

Ultimate Victory Formula: The feelings you feel, the thoughts you think, and the words you speak determine the life you live. The formula for this is: F+T+W=L

Victory Clock: An empowering way to view your alarm clock.

TIMELINE

From Three-Time Cancer Conqueror to the Seven Continent Marathon Man

Timeline of Matt's Victory Over Insurmountable Odds

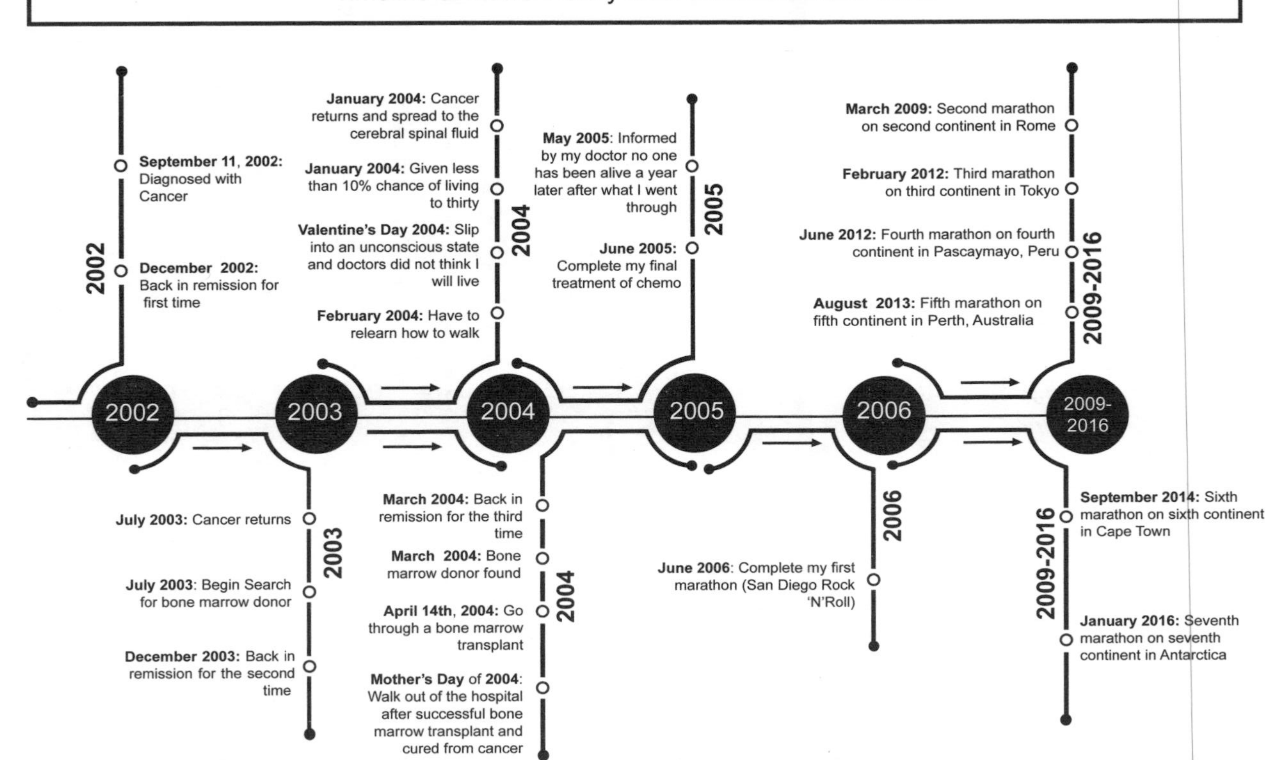

Special FREE Bonus Gift for You

To inspire you to achieve more victory, there are FREE **BONUS RESOURCES** for you at:

www.FreeGiftFromMatt.com

- Three free in-depth training videos for you on how to stay fired-up, pumped-up, and inspired to overcome adversity and achieve greater victory
- Free downloadable audio training with Matt Jones being interviewed by legendary speaker Les Brown guarantee bring you new ideas for success

ABOUT MATT

Matt Jones is considered one of the top keynote inspirational and motivational leadership speakers in the world.. He went from being a three-time cancer conqueror to relearning how to walk, to going through a bone marrow transplant, to running marathons around the world. Matt was diagnosed with cancer on September 11, 2002. After spreading to the fluid in his brain doctors did not think he would live. After victoriously conquering cancer he was told by his doctor that no one has gone through what he went through and been alive one year later.

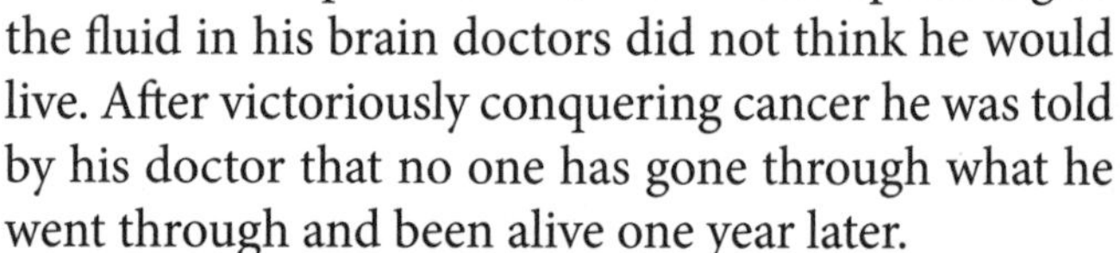

One year after finishing his last treatment of chemotherapy, Matt completed his first marathon. Baseball Hall of Famer George Brett said, "Matt is a true champion and his story inspires others to be a true champion." Matt is the the founder of the R.E.A.L Leadership Academy and the author of numerous books. Upon hearing Matt speak individuals and organizations are fired up, pumped up and inspired to overcome challenges and achieve greater victory in life, business, and leadership.

www.MatthewDJones.com